No One Needs Another Company **Mug**

Stop Branding and Start Experiencing

By

Lindsay Smith

ISBN: 979-8-9924048-0-7
Printed in the United States
First Edition

Published by Amplify Experiences, LLC
Springfield, Pennsylvania
www.amplify-experiences.com

This book is dedicated to my three children, who are the reason I do everything.

Audrina Brooklynn, Nathan Robert, & Hudson Charles.

"The purpose of life is to live it, to taste experience to the utmost, to reach out eagerly and without fear for newer and richer experience."—Eleanor Roosevelt

Nathan Robert (12), Audrina Brooklynn (13) & Hudson Charles (12).
Summer 2024.

Table of Contents

Introduction:

We all have one—an overflowing cabinet filled with company-branded mugs. Each is marked with the logo of a company we've worked with, yet none of them really stand out. We hold on to them, not because they hold sentimental value, but because throwing them out feels wasteful. Sure, one might keep your coffee a little warmer or be great for travel, but do any of them truly connect you back to the company? I'd bet you don't think, "I should go back to XYZ because they gave me a great mug."

If you're anything like me, when we look for recommendations, it's not the companies that showered us with swag that come to mind. Why? Because the secret to building lasting relationships—and turning one-time customers into loyal, repeat clients—lies not in the promotional products or clever branding but in the experiences companies create for their employees and customers. I know this firsthand, having spent over 20 years crafting these experiences, both for others and for myself.

In 2015, I was tasked with building a new region for my company, starting from scratch. Over the next nine years, that region would grow exponentially—not through massive marketing campaigns, glossy brochures, or branded giveaways, but through the power of relationships, experiences, and word-of-mouth referrals from employees and partners. By year six, we had reached $17.3 million in annual revenue. When I left the company in early 2024, the region had cumulatively generated over $82 million in revenue.

After my departure, I was flooded with messages from colleagues, partners, and clients expressing their gratitude. Every single one of them pointed to the relationships and experiences we had shared—not a single one mentioned a mug, a pen, or any other branded item. Instead, they spoke of how the experiences we created together were the driving force behind our success. And it wasn't by accident. It happened because I was intentional about creating exceptional experiences—both for the people I worked with and for the clients we served.

For me, everything comes down to one word: experiences. In fact, it's my favorite word in the English language. Over the years, I've often joked that I should write a book about all the experiences I've had, but I was never sure how to capture the essence of what I had learned. Then it hit me—this book should be about those very experiences. The ones that influenced not only company growth but also turned me into a loyal advocate for the brands I encountered. My hope is that as you read, you'll discover insights you can apply to your own business, helping you better connect with and impact your customers.

Far too many businesses focus solely on the "must-haves" and the "should-haves," but few pay attention to the "nice-to-haves." Here's the reality: when choosing between vendors, the basics are usually the same. You expect that a hotel will have a bed and a bathroom. You expect clean sheets. But no one raves about a hotel simply because it had a bed or clean sheets. Instead, they tell stories about the handwritten welcome note at check-in or the complimentary bottle of their favorite wine waiting in their room. Similarly, no one chooses a car dealership because they handed out mugs. But they will remember the dealership that created a custom simulation of how their new car would look parked in their driveway or who took a photo as they waved goodbye to their old car. These small, unexpected gestures are the "nice-to-haves" that create meaningful experiences. And it's those experiences that foster relationships, which, in turn, drive business growth.

This book is built on the idea that while anyone can build a brand, it takes a special touch to create experiences that surprise, delight, and ultimately build long-lasting relationships with your customers.

In this book, I'll share with you the strategies I used, along with the experiences that inspired me along the way. You'll find practical tips, creative ideas, and proven techniques that, when implemented thoughtfully, will set you apart from your competition. I'll also share how I've applied these same principles in my personal life, leading to deeper relationships and more memorable moments. Because the truth is, experiences don't just impact your business—they can enrich every aspect of your life.

A wise man once told me, "Work isn't meant to be the perfect life. Work is meant to fund the perfect life." Over the years, I've learned that blending meaningful experiences into both your professional and personal worlds is the key to achieving fulfillment in both.

This book is broken down into three sections. Each focuses on the art of customer experience through unique perspectives and examples that you can easily apply to your own business.

Section One: We'll start by diving into three brands that I believe excel in creating exceptional customer experiences. These brands don't just sell products or services; they build connections with their customers in ways that feel personal, meaningful, and unforgettable. Through their stories, you'll see how the power of experience can turn a one-time customer into a lifelong ambassador.

Section Two: Next, I'll share real-life examples from my own journey. As we launched a new region for my previous company, I had the opportunity to experiment with different strategies designed to foster deeper customer connections. In this section, you'll see how these methods contributed to significant growth, and you'll understand how the little details can make a world of difference when scaling a business.

Section Three: Finally, the third section of the book is designed specifically for you. Here, I'll outline ten easy-to-implement ideas that will help you create memorable experiences for your customers. These ideas don't require massive budgets or complicated processes—they just need a little creativity, empathy, and genuine interest in your clients. When done right, these strategies will not only delight your customers but also help your business grow in meaningful ways.

By the end of this book, you will have a deeper understanding of how creating experiences—rather than relying on branding alone—can transform your business. Whether you are just starting or looking for ways to reinvigorate your approach, these insights will give you the tools to take your customer relationships to the next level—all without another company mug.

Section 1

The Power of Brands That Build Experiences

In a world where customers are bombarded with brands vying for their attention, true success doesn't come from branding alone—it comes from creating experiences. When we think of brands, we often imagine their logos, taglines, and advertising campaigns. But the truth is, the most successful brands are those that prioritize creating unforgettable customer experiences. These experiences are what differentiate them in a crowded marketplace and keep customers coming back for more, especially in a time when clients crave connection, personalization, and moments that leave lasting impressions.

In this section, I'll explore three brands that don't just excel in branding—they shine in the way they make their customers feel. These companies have mastered the art of personal connection, turning transactions into memorable moments that build loyalty. You'll learn how each brand has made customer experience a cornerstone of its strategy, and how you can draw inspiration from their approaches to enhance your own business.

KIMPTON, AN IHG BRAND

The Kimpton Revelation: A New Standard in Experience

As an IHG Diamond Elite and Kimpton Inner Circle Member, my loyalty to the brand runs deep, but it wasn't always this way. Prior to 2013, I had little knowledge of Kimpton. In fact, when my mother first suggested I try a Kimpton property, I looked at her as though she had lost her mind. It wasn't that I doubted her judgment—she had impeccable taste—I just couldn't imagine hosting an event with any chain that wasn't what I considered a major brand. That was until a simple suggestion from her led to one of the most powerful customer experiences of my life, transforming not just how I viewed hospitality but also how I understood the importance of creating deep, meaningful relationships in business. What I learned, besides that I should always listen to my mother, was that the power of a brand can be transformed by the customer experience. What started as a blind trust in my mother's suggestion turned into one of the most powerful customer experiences of my life, perhaps even the one moment that changed forever how I would look at developing relationships.

That shift started with a man named Travis.

It was 2013, and there was a large event happening in Phoenix early the following year. I went out to scout locations to host a sub-party that we would have during the event. In advance of planning my trip, I researched a few different venues online. I learned that Kimpton's Palomar Hotel had just opened downtown, so I decided to check it out along with a few other venues. Upon arrival at the Palomar, I was greeted by name by the front desk. It was the first time I had ever stepped foot in Arizona, and I knew nothing about the city and very little about the property I was scouting. I assumed the warm welcome and knowing who I was could be attributed to the fact that I had given Travis my arrival time and was the only person in the lobby at the time. It felt great to be acknowledged. I checked into the room they had graciously comped for me, and after a brief chat with the front desk staff about the amenities, I went to the elevator to go up to my room.

When I opened the door, I walked in and on the small wooden table near the window, I found a handwritten note card from the team, a bottle of red wine, a bottle of white wine, and a tray with fruit and cheeses. Next to the bed, there were earplugs with a note letting me know there would be construction on the condos above the hotel, so if I wanted some extra silence, they provided the earplugs for my stay. I remember changing and taking the elevator down to the living room of the Kimpton Palomar in Phoenix, where I had scheduled a meeting with their event coordinator to walk through the space and discuss ideas.

The Power of Personalization: Building Loyalty Through Experience

As I got off the elevator, I was greeted by a man who, I later found out, was the hotel's General Manager. He said without hesitation, "Lindsay, it is so wonderful to have you here. Please let me know what I can do to make your stay better." I couldn't help but smile from ear to ear and wondered if I was on candid camera. I had no idea how this was possible. I met Travis at our designated spot, shared my experience with him—and he just smiled. We walked the site, he shared his ideas about how to bring my theme to life, and then we talked about the other venues I was considering. He shared positive feedback on the other venues, made suggestions about what I should look for, and even arranged for transportation—at the hotel's expense—for me to get to and from the venues for my site visits the next day.

The next day, I visited three other venues. These visits were a stark contrast to my Kimpton experience: cold, impersonal, and purely transactional. The venue representatives barely engaged, stuck to standard scripts, and offered no sense of connection or personal touch. I couldn't recall a single person's name from those visits, and, as far as I remember, I never received a follow-up from them. These venues gave me a few pens, a water bottle, a comped meal—which they didn't join me for—and a T-shirt with the venue name on it—all of which I think I left at the Kimpton. It became evident that while these venues were aesthetically impressive, they lacked what Kimpton had already delivered in spades—a focus on experience over space.

Upon my return to the property, my Kimpton contact and I met for appetizers and cocktails to debrief and for me to share my thoughts and feedback. I remember they served these amazing tater tots, handmade with bacon and chives and a slightly spicy dipping sauce. I shared with Travis that my experience at Kimpton couldn't have been more different from my site visits to other locations. Between the personal attention, the focus on my event vision, and the overall experience created during this site visit, I knew that Kimpton would easily create core memories for the attendees. And while the other venues were aesthetically pleasing, they were simply event spaces. I remember telling him that if they could serve the tater tots for 500 people, it was a done deal.

As we were getting ready to part ways, I just had to know how they were so spot-on from the start. So I asked Travis how it was possible that everyone knew who I was at Kimpton. He revealed that he had scoured my LinkedIn profile, printed my picture, and posted it in the staff area with my name and a "VIP" tag. I couldn't help but laugh, but it worked. I felt seen, valued, and special. And that feeling extended throughout my entire experience.

The event, held in February of 2014, was a roaring success—did I mention it was a 1920s theme? We had a big brass band, feather boas, pearls, fresh flowers, a photo booth, gaming tables, and the logo for the company I worked for at the time shining in bright lights on the side of the building—an element that guests remember to this day. They did, in fact, make the tater tots for the event and shortly thereafter removed them from the menu due to the intensity required to make them. They were replaced with polenta fries, made with the same ingredients and sauce—which I equally enjoyed for many years until the next menu change.

Going the Distance – The Secret to Repeat Business

My travels took me to Phoenix about 100 times after that, and every time, without fail—the front staff greeted me by name—because we became family. I'd find myself engaged in conversations with Cody at the front desk and with Jeremy, the manager. They would ask about my travels, my business meetings, and we'd talk about places we wanted to visit and experiences we'd had. They were nothing but gracious and always addressed me by name.

The important thing to remember is that to have a loyal customer base, you have to keep going back to the beginning. Looking back, Kimpton's emphasis on the experience didn't end after my first visit. One visit, I walked in and was told my room was upgraded, and on the table in the living area, I found three jars of treats with kindness tags and a note from the hotel telling me to pay it forward. I had so much fun walking through the city and handing out the jars to people I had never met before.

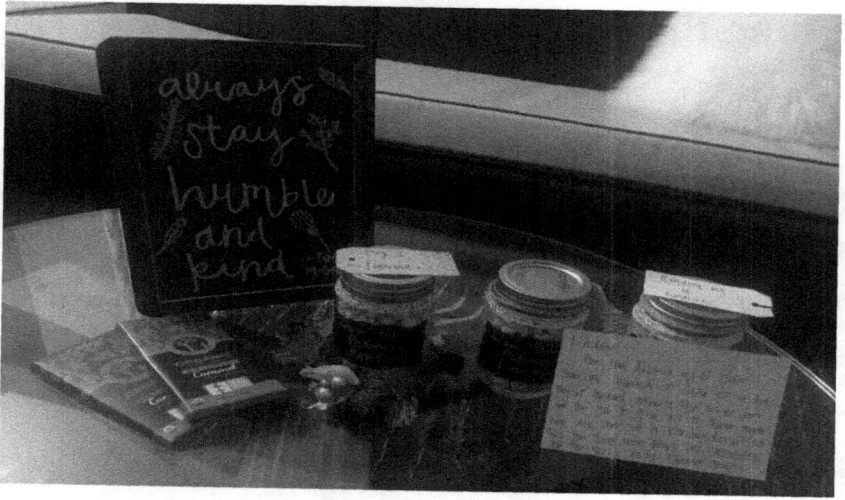

The Kindness Jars left for my by the Kimpton Palomar in Phoenix.

On yet another visit, I walked into my room in Phoenix and saw a Philadelphia Phillies banner on the wall, a pound cake with fresh berries and homemade whipped cream on the table, a chilled bottle of my favorite wine, a dozen roses in a vase by the bed, lavender linen spray on my pillow, a record player with a Luke Bryan record sitting on a chair, caramel candy on the nightstand, and a Phillies makeup purse in the bathroom. Every corner held another surprise for me. All of those items would have been nice on their own, but each of them connected directly to me. I'm from Philadelphia, and the Phillies had just had an exceptional run. My favorite dessert is pound cake with whipped cream and berries. I love a chilled glass of Sauvignon Blanc (from New Zealand or Sancerre—and this one was from New Zealand). My favorite scent is lavender, and fresh flowers always make me smile. As for music, I'm a country girl and, for the longest time, had the biggest crush on Luke Bryan. So the experience the Kimpton team created was personal; it was for me, and it had nothing to do with them, their brand, or what they had lying around.

These experiences weren't about Kimpton promoting their brand or flaunting what they could offer. It was about making me feel seen. It was about creating memories and deepening the connection with me as a guest.

One year, I was in town for my birthday, and my room was filled with the most gorgeous lavender flower arrangements, chocolate-covered strawberries, and a bottle of wine. Regardless of when I visited or what was happening, there was always a handwritten note from the front desk—and it was always personal to me. Each visit was another chapter in the evolving relationship I had with Kimpton.

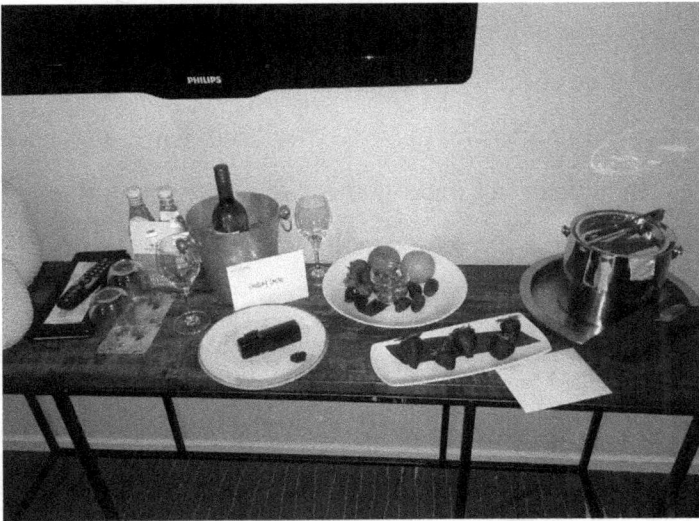

One of many welcome spreads in my suite at the Kimpton Palomar Phoenix, complete with a personal note.

Each time I stepped foot into a Kimpton, an experience was created. And with each experience, a relationship was deepened. Through these deepened relationships, brand loyalty was built, driving repeat business. Repeat business from a loyal customer adds profit to the bottom line in a much more sustainable way. In the Kimpton example, and the over 100 times I traveled to Phoenix, they didn't need to spend money on marketing—they spent nominal dollars, relative to what I spent, to create experiences that would make me continue to come back and think, "I wonder what is in store for me this time?" Sometimes it would just be a note and an upgraded room; other times, it would be an elaborate display of my favorite treats. And still other times, it would be an unexpected conversation with Cody, a Kimpton team member who remembered me and referenced specific things we spoke about on a previous trip. The staff was truly listening—they weren't just there to do a job, but rather to enhance the lives of those who came into their hotel. It is important to realize that personalization of an experience isn't just about giving clients what they want but making them feel seen and valued. Throwing my favorite bottle of wine on the table without a note wouldn't have the same impact. Remembering that I was visiting a sister property in Seattle and asking me how my stay was—that's making me feel incredibly seen.

Through these personalized moments, Kimpton taught me that loyalty isn't built through flashy ads or gimmicks. It's built through consistency, attention to detail, and making people feel truly valued. They didn't need to spend millions on marketing to keep me coming back. They simply created experiences that made me look forward to my next stay, each time wondering, "What surprise is waiting for me this time?" As a businessperson, I've taken those lessons and applied them to my professional life. In every venture, I now focus on creating meaningful relationships—much like Kimpton did with me—because I've seen firsthand how the power of personalization can turn a customer into a raving fan.

In a 2014 *Harvard Business Review* article titled "The Value of Customer Experience, Quantified," it's noted that customers with the highest customer experience ratings are 2.4 times more likely to become repeat customers. This is exactly what Kimpton did—they didn't just create customers; they created loyalty. And in doing so, they transformed me from a skeptical guest into a lifelong advocate.

The Zipper Incident: Turning a Wardrobe Malfunction into a Memorable Experience

In January of 2022, I was back in Phoenix for my first trip of the year. I had mastered the art of quick changing and had 30 minutes to transform from "Airport" Lindsay to "Let's Lead a Meeting" Lindsay. It was a new year, so naturally, I bought myself a new dress to wear and cut the tags off as soon as I unpacked it from my suitcase. As is typical, I was talking on the phone, doing my makeup, and trying to get dressed all at the same time—to maximize what I was able to accomplish, of course. As I slipped on my dress, I twisted my body into a pretzel to get the zipper up in the back, and that's when it happened—the zipper broke. It didn't just get stuck; it broke mid-zipper while on my body. So here I am, alone in my hotel room, watching the clock tick. Fifteen minutes to go. I wiggled myself, sucked everything in, and contorted in ways that only Cirque du Soleil performers can contort (okay, maybe the contortions were in my mind)—you get the picture. I was contemplating finding a pad of butter to grease myself out of the dress when I finally nudged it just enough to get the dress off. Having survived this New Year wardrobe malfunction, I thankfully had an extra dress, which I pulled from my suitcase. Note to anyone reading: always pack an extra dress when traveling for such occasions.

Five minutes to go. On a whim, I texted the front desk and asked if there was anyone who could replace a zipper overnight. They responded that they didn't think so, but they would check. I continued getting ready, and as I was about to walk out of the door, the hotel manager called up to my room to let me know that he would personally pick up my dress, take it to a seamstress he found, and wait to see if she could repair it. He said she couldn't make promises, as it was more complicated than just fixing a zipper and depended on the fabric. I was gracious and thought it was worth a shot. While I was in my meeting, less than two hours after my original inquiry, I received the following text:

"Zipper is all repaired. Is it okay to have someone bring the dress to your room and hang it in the closet? – Nate"

Was it okay? Was it okay to have someone take my dress, repair my dress, and return my dress all before my meeting ended? Heck yeah, it was. I told him to leave the receipt so I could pay for it, and he let me know that there would be no charge. Now, I wasn't at a dry cleaner's or a seamstress's business—I was at a hotel. While I can think of one or two other super-luxury brands that would do something like this for their clients, most hotel chains would not. Most hotels would have made the call and said they didn't have a seamstress in-house and maybe referred me to a local dry cleaner. But the Kimpton team went above and beyond again, and they did it all for me. So while the Kimpton fairies were working their magic, I was working my magic with my team in the office. And though I learned the next morning that the new zipper also didn't work (I blame it on the dress material), I couldn't stop thinking about how the Kimpton team yet again went out of their way for me—as I can guarantee that "How to help a guest who gets stuck in a dress before a meeting" isn't in their training manual.

I shared the experience of the zipper with my team as an example of going above and beyond to ensure that their clients were satisfied, even if it meant doing something outside of their business line. The hotel wasn't in the seamstress business; however, they saw a need and a way to make a very loyal client even more of a raving fan, and they jumped on it.

The Flowers Experiment

My business partner, Jim Campbell, was in the room for that meeting and said he wanted to prove that the Kimpton Hotel Brand goes above and beyond without question. He also became a Kimpton convert after attending that 2014 event. He would comment to me as we booked travel plans that every time, without fail, Kimpton had everything in its place, and it had come to feel like his second home. He told the team he was going to do a real-life, unscripted experiment. He then texted the Kimpton Palomar Phoenix, letting them know that he and I had a disagreement and that he felt bad. (He too had developed some deep personal relationships with the staff.) He asked if they would be able to pick up some flowers and place them in my room as a surprise for when I returned. He told the team he'd have me report back on what happened next.

When I got back to my room, I found flowers and a handwritten note—which Jim had dictated to them—sitting on my table. There was a Fry's next door to the hotel, so I imagine what happened is one of their team members ran out, grabbed the flowers, wrote the note, and placed it in my room. The gesture likely cost them under $10—and it continued to build brand loyalty for both myself and Jim. And to be clear, there never was a fight - but nonetheless, the Kimpton Team delivered.

The Compound Effect of Experiences

Since then, I've spent time at Kimpton Hotels in Cleveland, Ohio; Fort Lauderdale, Florida; Vero Beach, Florida; Sedona, Arizona; Philadelphia, Pennsylvania; New York, New York; Atlanta, Georgia; Savannah, Georgia; and Seattle, Washington, to name a few. The consistency in the service level and the experience created remain constant. At every front desk, I'm greeted and recognized as a VIP. It's obvious that the customer profile they have on me travels with me—my favorite candies, wines, and treats are waiting for me in my room along with a handwritten note card every time—in every city. They aren't generic—they are personal to me. It shows me that the systems they have in place to assure consistency and personalization work, and every single time it causes me to smile.

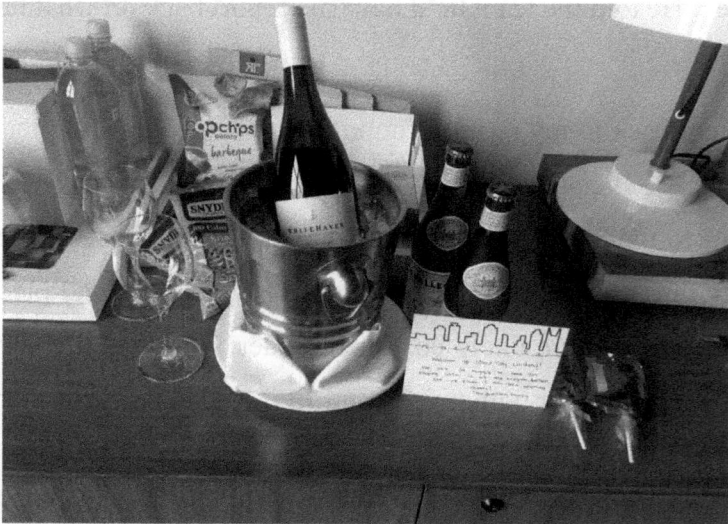

I was greeted in Nashville by the Kimpton Aertson Hotel with a warm, personalized welcome. My preferences followed me all the way from Phoenix.

I refer my friends and family to Kimpton. A recent college roommate and children's summer vacation landed us at the Kimpton in Vero Beach, and the entire team went above and beyond to make sure all 18 of us were taken care of from the moment we stepped foot onto the property. They moved all of our rooms to be next to one another, taking up a considerable portion of the floor. They delivered wines and chocolates to all of our rooms, filled our fridges with the food we ordered on Instacart, and brought up larger trash cans when asked. The experience, coupled with my endless Kimpton stories, converted at least one of the families to Kimpton fans. I'm pretty sure we already have our next trip booked, too.

I don't even want to guesstimate how much money I've spent at the Kimpton properties since that first meeting in 2013. I've probably logged 500+ nights collectively at their properties over the last nine years. That doesn't include the nights those I've referred to Kimpton have spent and the other events I've hosted at one of their properties. Travis didn't know at that first meeting the possible scope of my value to Kimpton; he just knew that he wanted to craft an experience unlike any other property to win the event. He did that, and more.

This attention to detail has made Kimpton more than just a hotel chain—it's become a part of my journey. Through their consistent dedication to crafting personalized experiences, Kimpton has not only earned my loyalty but has shaped how I approach building relationships, in both business and life.

In today's world, where personalization often feels automated and forced, Kimpton stands out as a reminder that real relationships are built on genuine care, attentiveness, and the smallest of thoughtful details. And that, in turn, creates a loyalty that can't be bought—only earned.

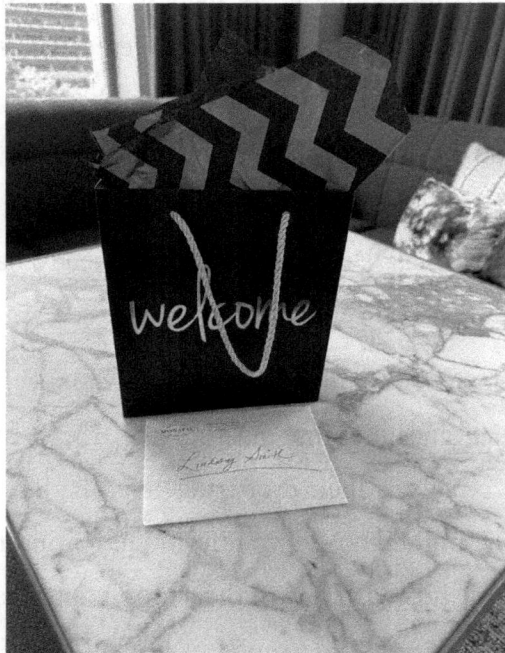

A personalized welcome greeting by the Kimpton Monaco in Philadelphia.

My own personal experiences deeply impacted my professional decisions and business growth, and over the years, we hosted a number of events at the Kimpton Hotel in Phoenix. Each one was tailored to make our guests feel like VIPs. We hosted employee dinners outside of the Blue Hound restaurant on a long table. We gave speeches recounting how, before we had offices in Phoenix, we had the Kimpton—and many of our first team members had interviews in the Kimpton's Living Room.

Unconventional, yes; effective, also yes. As business grew, we did seminars for clients, complete with floral arrangements, handwritten, personal notes of gratitude upon the guests' arrival, and catered lunches. These weren't typical classes—they had uplighting, stages, and elevated menus. We wanted our clients to understand that we wanted them to feel like VIPs—just as Travis had first made me feel. At the end of the seminar, we'd host private masterminds with our speakers and a handful of guests. They'd be treated to wine service, a wonderful dinner, impeccable service, and some high-level conversations. Aesthetically, the rooms were gorgeous. We'd repurpose flowers, have another set of custom thank-yous, and a personalized gift for each attendee. All of these things were small ways of deepening the relationships that we had with our clients—and therefore growing our businesses.

The investment into the events helped us to have personalized opportunities to have conversations outside of a business setting and at more personal levels. We spoke about families, ideas, and growth.

As our team grew, we moved our employee dinners to this really cool room off the pool—they'd remove furniture, put tables together, cover them in linens, and allow us to make the space our own. We brought in musicians, had signature drinks, and lots of smiles. A mentor of mine said to me years ago, "If you want the team to give Ritz Carlton Service, have you considered that they might never have been to a Ritz Carlton?" That phrase stuck with me, and it was critical to our success that not only our clients were treated to a Kimpton experience, but also our team members. We built a culture that wasn't like any other company in the space—we built a culture where our team members were able to experience VIP dinners and have conversations and cocktails with some of the company's executives. We'd use those environments to talk about evolving as a company or overcoming challenges. We'd connect on personal levels so that our team members became connected more deeply than just people who worked together.

In 2021, post-pandemic, we had an opportunity to host a large event for 80 of our team members, many of whom had never been to Phoenix, for three days. This was the first time our Eastern Division was visiting our Western Division. By this point, it had expanded past Arizona and included New Mexico, Washington, Idaho, and Alaska. The Kimpton Palomar Phoenix allowed us to take over the hotel and brand it completely for us. Off the elevator, we had floor tiles with our core values, which we also wrapped around the pool columns.

We brought in the Regional Manager for Kimpton, who was based out of one of their properties in Chicago, and he explained to us how they brand and how the Kimpton team creates Kimpton moments. I thought it was so smart—and I had witnessed and experienced them throughout my visits within the Kimpton family. I had this nagging feeling inside of me the entire time that he spoke saying, "If businesses focused on the experience vs. the product or the service—their revenues would skyrocket."

Now, while Kimpton's business is hospitality, the company I worked for wasn't in the business of hospitality. But we were able to leverage the hospitality experiences we created to grow our real estate service business at a drastic rate in a short period of time. At the end of the day, we were selling an insurance policy—but the brand loyalty to us as a partner and to our companies was attributed directly to the relationships formed along the way. In conversations over the years with partners, I asked what made them choose us and what made them stay—even when things were difficult. They all said similar things: "It was the relationship that we had." "It was your genuineness." "It was the way you always showed up." "It was the way you made us feel." Our focus on the experience is what drew clients and partners to us, like a magnet, and allowed our remarkable teams to serve them at the highest level possible.

The Kimpton Schofield in Cleveland welcomed me with lavender linen spray, purple flowers, wine, sparkling water, popcorn and chocolate candies.

Raving Fans

According to the *Inc.* article, "The Secret Ratio that Proves Why Customer Reviews are So Important," published in 2018, it takes approximately 40 positive customer reviews to overcome one negative employee review. The best way to increase positive employee reviews—whether formal or informal, through word of mouth—is to create such positive experiences that the recipient wants to share. Having surveyed over 10,000 clients during my tenure at my previous company, I'm aware that the people who feel the need to share their experiences most often are those who have had negative experiences. But when you create an environment with team members and a culture that allows for memorable experiences to happen for customers—think about my zipper at the Kimpton or the way Travis secretly taught everyone to call me by my name the first time they met me—you're putting positive energy out, which will cause a ripple effect in your business. It's about focusing on the "nice-to-haves" and not just the basic requirements of your business.

Those nice-to-haves have earned Kimpton a considerable amount of business—they helped my former company to grow at astronomical rates, and they can help your business do the same.

The Kimpton experience taught me to focus on surprising, delighting, and personalizing every experience.

PIERI HOSPITALITY

Pieri Hospitality – Delivering Experiences Beyond the Menu

Sometime close to a decade ago, I needed to plan an event that would be unlike anything my team had ever experienced, one that would break the proverbial "conference dinner mold." I didn't want just another dinner—I wanted to create something the guests would remember for years to come. That's when I turned to Christina Pieri, Brian Pieri, Will Langlois, John Mathas, and Ally Bompartito of Pieri Hospitality, whose restaurants had already made an impression on me with their warmth and creativity. I suggested the idea of a wine pairing event, but what they delivered far exceeded my expectations, and it set the tone for a relationship that would inspire both personal loyalty and professional insights into the power of customer-centric experiences.

The Pieri team crafted an "Old World vs. New World" wine pairing event, with each wine thoughtfully curated to showcase the differences between tradition and innovation in winemaking. But the event was about much more than just wine. They gave us exclusive access to Bar Lucca, reserving the entire first floor and patio, turning the restaurant into our private haven for the evening. The open glass doors let in the cool autumn breeze, creating an ambiance that felt both intimate and expansive. As I mingled with my guests, many of whom were from out of town, I could see that this event was different. Conversations flowed as freely as the wine, and excitement was in the air. Guests who had never been particularly interested in wine were suddenly engaged, discussing the nuances of each pour as Chef Will kept an endless stream of pizzas and delicacies coming from the brick oven. It was more than just a dinner—it was a shared experience that bonded us all.

Looking back, this event taught me a critical lesson in business: when you create an experience that touches people on a personal level, they remember you, and they return to you. The Pieri team didn't just serve food; they created a space where connections flourished, where people felt valued and engaged. In the world of business, this translates to the importance of prioritizing relationships over transactions. Pieri Hospitality understands this intuitively. Every interaction with them feels less like a business deal and more like the fostering of a long-term relationship—a value that successful businesses must cultivate if they want to thrive.

The open air kitchen at Bar Lucca complete with a pizza oven on the night of our event.

Experiences that Shape Lifelong Loyalty

In 2017, my daughter Audrina turned seven. At the time, I was traveling for business, and while I was away, my parents took her to a pasta-making class at Cerdo (now Bar Sera). I received a text from my mom saying that Audrina wanted her birthday party to be just like the class she had attended. Knowing how much she loved the experience, I reached out to Christina to see if we could make this dream a reality. The answer was an immediate "yes." Christina and Chef Will were not only willing to recreate the class but eager to take it to the next level.

This birthday party was no ordinary event. Chef Will didn't just teach the children how to make pasta; he created an immersive culinary experience where 20 seven-year-olds got hands-on with dough, shaping and cutting it themselves. There was excitement in the room as the kids flourished under the guidance of someone who genuinely cared about their experience. The second floor of Bar Lucca was transformed into a pasta workshop, and the kids took pride in what they made. This wasn't just about creating food; it was about giving these children an unforgettable moment. To commemorate the event, we gave each child a custom pizza cutter engraved with "Audrina Brooklynn's 7th Birthday"—a small detail that added an extra layer of meaning to the day.

What struck me most about this experience was how the Pieri team went beyond the transactional elements of hosting a party. They could have easily offered a pre-set birthday package, something simple and profitable. But instead, they focused on crafting a memory. This is a key differentiator in business: when companies prioritize creating memorable experiences over simply delivering a product or service, they foster deep, emotional connections with their customers. This, in turn, drives loyalty. The party wasn't just a success because it was fun—it was successful because it was meaningful. It became a part of our family's narrative, and because of that, Pieri Hospitality became a part of our entire family's lives in a lasting way.

My birthday girl, Audrina, and Chef Will making homemade pasta at her 7th birthday party.

Connecting the Experience to Business Growth

What I realized over time is that this philosophy of creating tailored, unique experiences is not just good customer service—it's a business growth strategy. In a competitive market, especially one as crowded as hospitality, standing out isn't just about having the best food or the most elegant venue. It's about the emotional resonance you create with your clientele. People remember how you make them feel, and when that feeling is one of being deeply valued, they return—again and again.

For businesses looking to grow, this is a critical takeaway. The customer experience needs to be designed with the individual in mind. Companies that take the time to understand their customers' desires, preferences, and even quirks are the ones that rise above the rest. This extends beyond hospitality—it applies to every business, from retail to technology. Whether you're selling a product or offering a service, what you're really selling is an experience.

I saw this firsthand when Pieri Hospitality helped me host a series of baseball tailgates. These events, which catered to about 700 people, could have easily become logistical nightmares, but the Pieri team made them feel effortless. When I asked for creative ideas, they didn't just deliver—they innovated. One year, I suggested serving everything "on a stick." Chef Will took that idea and ran with it, producing a gourmet menu where every item was skewered, transforming a simple tailgate into a culinary adventure. Each year, they crafted a new menu based on my ideas, and it always exceeded expectations—and left the guests talking. And while we'd always serve wine and beer, John always brought a secret stash of my favorite Sancerre wine to serve to me. It was silly—we were paying for the wine, but the fact that he remembered and brought it made all the difference to me. And I'm not the only one. The Pieri team listens and remembers, using conversations and moments to create experiences for their guests. In my case, the crowd experienced tailgates like they never had before—and the Pieri touches complemented the other elements of the day—truly making it feel like a VIP experience and not just another baseball tailgate.

A personalized, upscale, and individual display at one of the tailgates catered by Pieri Hospitality. Veggies and hummus, individual charcuterie cups, street corn salad and cookies with cannoli dip were among a few of the delicacies served.

The lesson here for businesses is clear: don't just meet your customers' expectations—anticipate them and then exceed them. When a customer feels like their needs are not only understood but also prioritized, they become more than a customer—they become an advocate. In my case, Pieri Hospitality didn't just win my business; they won my loyalty. I became an advocate for their brand, referring friends and colleagues, and returning for more because they had proven time and again that they were invested in my experience.

Creating Emotional Connections in Business

The most striking example of this came when I turned 40. A lifelong dream of mine had been to visit Paris, but when that wasn't possible, I decided to bring a little piece of Paris to me. I approached the Pieri team with the idea of transforming their Italian restaurant, Bar Sera, into a Parisian haven for the evening. This was a tall order, but once again, they not only accepted the challenge—they embraced it wholeheartedly.

Chef Will crafted a French-inspired menu that rivaled anything you might find in the heart of Paris. The restaurant was transformed into an elegant, European-style bistro, complete with a grazing table that invited guests to mingle and indulge as though they were gathered at a street-side café. The ambiance, the food, the wine—it was all perfect. But what made the evening truly special was the feeling that this wasn't just a birthday party; it was an experience crafted uniquely for me.

This personal touch is something every business should strive to achieve. In today's market, where consumers are constantly bombarded with options, the companies that stand out are the ones that make their customers feel seen, heard, and valued. The Pieri team understood that my 40th birthday wasn't just about celebrating—it was about creating a moment that resonated on a deeper level. They didn't just deliver food and wine; they delivered a memory.

And that memory and those experiences translated into more business three years later. One of my best friends is now throwing her daughter's Sweet Sixteen— with a very different theme than Paris, as you can imagine—at Bar Sera. Why? Because she and her husband were guests at my 40th, and her husband fell in love with the attention to detail, the quality of the food, and the way he, as a guest, felt at the party and wanted to deliver that same experience to his daughter, her friends, and guests.

In my Parisian Haven created by Bar Sera on my 40th Birthday.

Customer Loyalty as a Business Growth Driver

My loyalty to the Pieri brand stems from their ability to continuously create these moments of emotional connection. And it's not just me—businesses that focus on cultivating these kinds of relationships see significant returns. According to a study by *Harvard Business Review*, customers who feel emotionally connected to a brand are far more valuable than highly satisfied customers—they spend more, stay longer, and refer others at a much higher rate. Funny, none of the business reviews mention customers referring business because of company swag—and yet that is what most companies use as their marketing efforts. It's not the things that create connection but rather the memory of the experience.

Pieri Hospitality's success is a testament to this. Their brand is not just built on the quality of their food or the elegance of their spaces; it's built on their ability to build relationships. Even in small moments, like the time I walked into Bar Lucca to pick up a takeout order and found the bag covered in Sharpie with the words "We Love Lindsay Smith," they demonstrate their commitment to making each interaction personal and meaningful.

In today's business landscape, where competition is fierce and customer loyalty is harder to secure, brands that prioritize building relationships over transactions are the ones that thrive. This is a strategy that businesses of all sizes and across all industries can adopt. By focusing on what makes customers feel valued, companies can turn one-time buyers into lifelong advocates.

Many brands say the customer is always right—few mean it. I ordered from a local catering company recently. The food was fine. The price was fine. But there was no experience—it was a transaction between party A and party B. The options were what was printed in black and white on their menu. It lacked emotion, it lacked experience, and it lacked understanding of their customers. In my experiences with Pieri Hospitality, they allow for creativity, conversation, and care about what the experience is like for you.

I walked in recently to one of their restaurants with a large group; Ally greeted me by name, and when I asked about outdoor seating, they said to give them five minutes. I walked out, and they had manifested a table large enough for my group of 10 outside on the patio—it was perfect. Service continued with the server calling me by name, allowing us to sample the wines before ordering, and being intimately aware of an allergy in our group, assuring that the experience for that guest was equal to or greater than the rest of the group. The experience was built on their desire to continue fostering a relationship—not a transaction. And yet again, relationships make huge differences.

This isn't something that applies just to hospitality. The way Pieri Hospitality runs their business is something that any business in any space should consider as a way to increase client bases and ticket sales. Consider the last time you had clients come into your office or store— how would the experience shift if you addressed them by name or anticipated their needs before they asked? The reality is, if schools taught students this—instead of segmenting customer lists and optimizing SEO—the power of personal referrals would be so great it could entirely change the way we do and grow businesses. I witnessed it firsthand as I developed our Western Region—no salespeople, no SEO optimization, no company Mugs—just an emphasis on an extreme customer, prospect, and employee experience to build loyalty.

More than a Restaurant

What the Pieri team did magically was create a following. They bought a farm, and through the farm, they deliver fresh vegetables to their restaurants but also allow the community to participate in their crops through a CSA. Weekly, I'd drive 30 minutes to pick up a box of vegetables from the farm. The secret—I didn't even like vegetables. Why did I do it? Because in each box, there was always a special creation from Chef Will. Maybe it was a seasoning or a dressing. Perhaps it was a suggestion for the best way to serve a particular item. Periodically, they curated a cookbook with recipes showcasing the vegetables they grew on the farm and included that in the box. And annually, they hosted their CSA members at the farm in Coopersburg for a tour to see where things came from and offered the option for a boxed lunch to sit on the farm, which I always opted in for. I envisioned events on the property and loved the sense of familiarity I found when walking their fields. I was hooked—not just to the food and the restaurants, but to the brand for the community that they created. And to this day, I still don't own a Pieri Mug, but they are absolutely top of mind when anyone asks for a recommendation for a restaurant, a catering company, an event space, or an experience.

Contents of some of the CSA Boxes fresh from Pieri Farm complete with Chef Will's surprise creations for members.

Innovation Brings Opportunities

When Pieri Farm was established, they planted a vineyard. For anyone who knows anything about wine—it takes a long time to grow grapes that can be produced into wine. And then it takes a long time to ferment and create the wine. I remember talking with John when they planted the grapes and discussing the ultimate wines they'd have. I always wondered why certain regions were known for certain wines. He shared that they ordered their vines from a nursery which grafted the varietals they wanted—Chardonnay, Viognier, Albariño, Cabernet Franc, Cabernet Sauvignon, Pinot Noir, and Barbera—with the root system from a varietal that would grow in the Pennsylvania climate and soil. For someone who enjoys wine like I do, I found this fascinating.

Each year, I'd watch the grapes grow, but I'd never see the wine. Patience was something I needed to have to see this project through—and I was only on the outside, so I can imagine what the Pieri team felt. I had contracted with Pieri Hospitality to do a wine pairing for a group of my colleagues, complete with one of Chef Will's handcrafted menus, for an event with some of our leaders. John shared that they had ordered their equipment to finally harvest and press the wine. The challenge was that harvesting lasts only a matter of days, and their equipment was stuck on a boat on its way from Italy.

As luck would have it, the equipment arrived, the grapes were harvested, and the wine was in production. It sounds a lot easier as I'm writing it than I know the process actually was, but the point is—it was in production.

A restaurant group that started with a single restaurant had innovated and expanded their portfolio to include multiple restaurants, a catering division, a farm, and now a vineyard. Through innovation, they were now exposed to new potential clients, as well as giving existing clients something new and exciting to look forward to being part of.

Their wine sales started in 2024—at a local farmer's market as well as inside their restaurants as part of their wine menus. So naturally, I made the 30-minute drive to catch them at one of their farmer's markets right before I went on my family vacation this year, picking up a few bottles to try while sitting poolside.

A crisp glass of Pieri Vineyard's Viognier is one of my personal favorite wines.

Typically, I would have gone to the local liquor store—but the excitement of trying their newest offering drew me in to them. So to Maryland I went, with bottles of Pieri's white wines clinking in my trunk. I had never had the wines, so it wasn't because I knew they were delicious (which, as it turns out, they are) but rather because I was excited to be a part of their history and eager to share the experience with my parents, whom I knew would also love the wine.

In fact, I was at a conference in Napa and was approached by a man from Georgia who was also at the event, and he was talking about wine production outside of the Northern California area. He was fascinated with the ways in which the same grapes taste based on climate and production styles. I shared with him about Pieri Vineyards, and he added it to the list of places he wanted to check out. So while somewhere on their farm harvesting grapes, Pieri Vineyards had business conversations happening across the country in Napa. It's a testament to the experience of having been able to watch the grapes when first planted and now knowing that they would finally be producing a harvest which would result in wines that could be shared.

Community Involvement

Brian Pieri did a Facebook post last year where he offered an opportunity for local Conshohocken children to become entrepreneurs. He donated pizza kits; kids were in charge of marketing and selling them. Was it to increase market share for his company? No. It was, rather, to give back to the community and to help the next generation of children understand what it was like to run a business. Brilliant. Flash forward a year later, I approached Brian about doing a similar event as a fundraiser for my daughter's 8th-grade class. We'd buy the kits at cost, and Brian would come to the school to teach the kids about being an entrepreneur and selling. They would present to the class, receive a grade, and pre-sell the kits. On delivery day, the kids would build the kits. This isn't on the Pieri Hospitality menu—but it's part of their experience. And above and beyond the life lessons these kids will learn, think about how many new potential customers will be exposed to the brand—because they will see the involvement of the students and therefore be exposed to the offerings of a hospitality group that they may previously not have known.

Showing up in communities is often seen as a "nice to have" versus a "must have." What would happen if you reviewed your annual marketing budget and found a way to support the community in some capacity? Who might you target, and what business is possible because of your involvement? I'm not suggesting that everyone gives money to put their company name on the back of a youth baseball jersey—because that isn't what I'm talking about when I say community involvement. I'm talking about something that creates an experience for people in the community—

sharing products or services at a flea market, coming through in a big way after a fire, contributing to the development of the next generation with life skills, offering something meaningful at a vendor fair—these are ways you can support the community and grow your business. If you took the same $500 that you would put toward your name on a baseball jersey and instead gave the team a pizza party after a big win, or gave each of them a custom water bottle, or put it toward a team-building experience for the kids—that would have a bigger impact on your business. The players would remember the experience, the parents would remember the experience, and your business would be top of mind when someone asked them for a referral. Community outreach is something that the Pieri team has mastered, and ultimately it's served them well.

Adapting to Change: The Pieri Hospitality Response to COVID-19

One of the most impressive aspects of Pieri Hospitality's approach is their adaptability, a critical trait for any business looking to sustain growth in the long term. When the COVID-19 pandemic hit, many businesses in the hospitality industry struggled to survive. But instead of retreating, the Pieri team pivoted. They introduced creative offerings like online wine-tasting classes, Father's Day grill boxes, and Mother's Day brunch kits to allow patrons to bring the Pieri experience home—all while helping to keep their team engaged and employed. They used social media in a very smart way to reach patrons who weren't out and about in the communities. They found ways to send the Pieri Hospitality experience home to you. Another way they proved that their brand wasn't their restaurants—it was the relationship they built. I distinctly remember one day in May of 2020 when my parents, aunt, and uncle joined me at my house. We signed onto the Zoom wine tasting, opened our wine boxes that I had picked up earlier, and joined with others— whom we had never met—for a shared experience led by John. Even when the world said, "you can't be together," the Pieri team found a way to craft an experience pulling people together from all different parts of the area—creating community and giving everyone positive memories.

When the state allowed for outdoor dining, they transformed their parking lot into an open-air dining establishment, allowing for the slow return of customers on site. They found ways to continue delivering value to their customers, even when traditional dining wasn't an option.

This adaptability speaks to a key lesson in business: the ability to pivot is crucial to growth. Companies that can respond to changes in the market, while still staying true to their core values, are the ones that emerge stronger. For Pieri Hospitality, the pandemic was an opportunity to reinforce their commitment to the community, offering a sense of connection in a time of isolation. Their ability to innovate in the face of adversity further strengthened their brand, proving that they were more than just a restaurant group—they were a pillar of support for their customers.

Pieri Hospitality's response to COVID-19, Father's Day Grill boxes allowing the community to take some of the Pieri goodness to their own kitchens.

Celebrating mom during COVID-19 with a Mother's Day Box from Pieri Hospitality complete with prosecco, chocolate dipped pizzelles, gold dusted strawberries and hand crafted gelato.

More than a Brand – A Family

I recently had the privilege of attending Pieri Hospitality's 15th anniversary celebration for their first restaurant, The StoneRose Restaurant. It was a Thursday evening in September, and the event was held in the very place where Pieri Hospitality began. The room was buzzing with energy, filled with people whose lives had been touched by this remarkable group. Old employees mingled with new ones, while loyal patrons exchanged stories about their time at the restaurant. Trays of hors d'oeuvres floated around the room, and in one corner, a display of photos hung from twine, showcasing Pieri's humble beginnings.

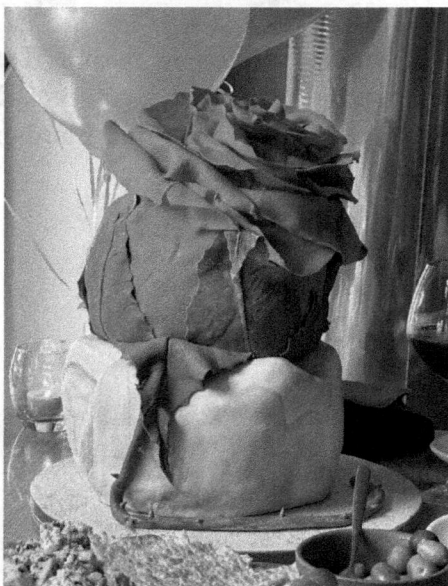

The exquisitely designed cake for The StoneRose Restaurant's 15th Anniversary Party that was displayed for guests to see upon their arrival.

Many of the faces in those early pictures still work with the company today, just a few years older.

I found myself standing by the door, taking in the scene, and I realized that this wasn't just a typical anniversary party. With Billy Joel playing softly in the background, it hit me: this wasn't an event to celebrate employees or even customers. This was a family reunion.

One of the first people I spoke with was Ally. She smiled and immediately asked about my kids—not just in passing, but with genuine curiosity, recalling every milestone in my life. She remembered my daughter's 7th birthday pasta party, my mom's 60th wine party, the pig roast we hosted for my husband's 40th birthday during COVID, and the soccer team luaus that Pieri Hospitality catered. Her attention to detail floored me. Ally didn't have to remember any of that, but she did, because that's what Pieri Hospitality is all about—it's about relationships that go beyond the transactional, creating a bond that feels like family.

As the evening progressed, I sat at the bar and met Dean and Franco, two regulars who have been coming to The StoneRose Restaurant every Wednesday and Thursday since it opened. They sit in the same seats each time, week after week. Though I had never met them before, we struck up hours of conversation as if we had known each other for years. That's the magic of a place like The StoneRose Restaurant; it turns strangers into friends and customers into extended family.

Toward the end of the night, Brian Pieri gave a brief but heartfelt speech, thanking everyone for being a part of the journey. A cake shaped like a rose atop a stone block was brought out and sliced, and John, everyone's favorite sommelier, poured vintage champagne for all the guests gathered around the bar. There was no pretense, no grand show—just genuine gratitude for the people who had helped shape Pieri Hospitality over the years.

John Mathas, Sommelier for Pieri Hospitality, opening a vintage bottle of Cava during The Stone Rose Restaurant's 15th Anniversary Party.

The entire evening was more than a celebration; it was an experience that spoke to the heart of what Pieri has built over the last 15 years. It was a reminder that this company isn't just about running a successful restaurant or catering business. It's about fostering relationships that endure the test of time. Each guest, whether they were a patron, an employee, or a friend of the family, added to the collective memory of Pieri Hospitality.

As I left that night, I realized that what Pieri had created was more than just a brand. It was a community. A family. And every person in that room was part of it. The event wasn't simply a marker of years past; it was a celebration of the connections made, the shared experiences, and the countless stories that form the foundation of what they do. This is what sets Pieri Hospitality apart—they don't just serve food; they serve moments that last a lifetime.

The Power of Experiences in Business Growth

The Pieri Experience is about more than just exceptional food and service; it's about crafting meaningful, emotional connections that leave a lasting impression. In business, this translates to the understanding that customer relationships are the foundation of growth. Whether it's through a birthday party, a wine pairing, or a large-scale tailgate, Pieri Hospitality has mastered the art of making every customer feel special. Their success is a powerful reminder that when you focus on creating experiences over transactions, loyalty and growth follow.

This philosophy is one that any business can adopt. By prioritizing relationships, anticipating needs, and continuously delivering value, companies can cultivate the kind of loyalty that drives long-term success. In the end, it's not just about what you sell—it's about how you make your customers feel. And when you make them feel valued, they will return to you time and time again.

HIGH MARK DISTILLERY

The High Mark Difference

I first met Felicia Keith-Jones in 2018 at a women's group in San Diego. It was a serendipitous encounter, one that felt fated from the start. After a few days of back-to-back meetings, our energies aligned, and we decided to take an afternoon break. We headed to Coronado Island's beaches, capturing photos of sandcastles, climbing on rocks by the ocean, and sharing our dreams of future adventures. Though we had only known each other for 48 hours, there was an unspoken connection between us—one rooted in a shared passion for creating experiences, pushing boundaries, and making a lasting impact.

By the time we co-planned a 2019 conference in Nashville, our bond was solidified. From the very beginning, we agreed on one guiding principle: the experience was everything. If we focused on creating a memorable, meaningful experience, we knew the rest would fall into place naturally. That philosophy, I would come to learn, is central to how Felicia operates in both life and business.

Felicia isn't just the Master Distiller for High Mark Distillery in Reno, Nevada; she is a trailblazer. The first female distiller in Alaska, the first female distiller in Nevada, one of only eight female distillers in America, and one of only a select few in the world. Impressive, right? Felicia's journey into the world of distilling is as fascinating as it is inspiring. Before founding High Mark in 2010, she spent years as a young teacher in Alaska's bush, as a bush pilot in Alaska, living abroad, and honing her craft by earning distillation credentials from Ireland. The distillery began with her uncle's Scottish Apple Jack recipe, a nod to her family's heritage.

But for Felicia, the spirits are just one part of the equation. What truly sets High Mark apart is its unwavering focus on creating extraordinary experiences for everyone who steps through their doors—whether they are customers, family, or friends.

At High Mark, you're not just buying a bottle of spirits; you're becoming part of a story, a legacy. One of the ways Felicia cultivates these deeper connections is through her exclusive Barrel Club, where members can become investors in the bourbon industry. As a Master Distiller, she offers classes where guests can learn how to make cocktails and spirits in a fun, interactive setting—and they can take the recipes learned home to recreate the High Mark experience with their friends and families. They also offer an intimate, hands-on experience that brings people closer to the craft, allowing them to take home something more than just a product—they leave with a memory, a bond, and a connection to the brand that extends beyond the label.

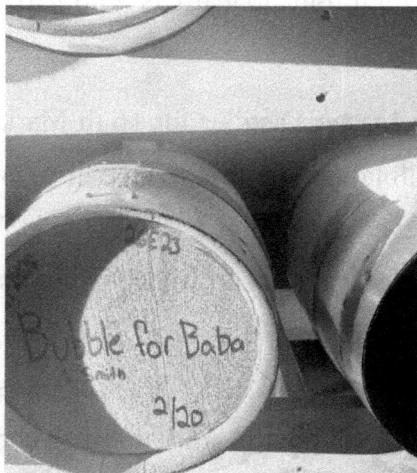

One of my personal bourbon barrels, named in honor of my late Baba, aging at High Mark Distillery in Reno, Nevada.

This focus on connection was beautifully demonstrated by a story Felicia shared with me during one of our many adventures. An elderly gentleman came into the distillery with his daughter. He was forgetful, repeatedly asking the same questions over and over. Yet, Felicia greeted him with the same warmth and patience she offers to everyone. The elderly man's daughter, moved by Felicia's kindness, expressed her gratitude for the way she treated her father. Felicia simply said it was her pleasure, never once making the man feel rushed or burdensome. Just two weeks later, after the man had passed, his daughter returned to the distillery. She came back not to buy more spirits but with tears in her eyes, she wanted to thank Felicia once again for the kindness she had shown. The memory of that afternoon, she said, had been one of the last truly joyful moments her father had enjoyed before his passing from severe Alzheimer's Disease.

The daughter didn't have to return, but she did—because what Felicia and her team had created went far beyond a transaction. It was a moment of deep human connection, one that left a lasting imprint on both the daughter and her elderly father. This story perfectly encapsulates what makes High Mark Distillery so unique: they don't just serve customers; they touch lives.

Private Labeling

When I was growing my region, I knew I could rely on Felicia's commitment to creating experiences that transcend her brand. I reached out to her, asking if she could craft a custom spirit for an upcoming camping-themed event. Instead of simply bottling one of her existing products, Felicia and her team got to work. They created a custom "S'mores" spirit, meticulously roasting huge trays of marshmallows, crushing hundreds of graham crackers, and pushing gallons of chocolate liquor through her stills. Once the blend was perfected, they hand-labeled each bottle with my company's logo and shipped them to the event, transforming a simple gift into a one-of-a-kind experience for each attendee to feel like they were truly on a camping trip during their conference.

This wasn't an isolated incident. Time and again, Felicia and her team have gone above and beyond to make each event, each bottle, and each encounter feel special. High Mark's graphic designer has custom-created labels that showcase the spirit's purpose rather than where it came from, shifting the focus from their own brand to the experience they are helping to create. We were proud to hand out truly customized gifts to our VIP attendees to let each of them know how special they are to us.

In 2024, I hosted a special event in Las Vegas at the luxurious Four Seasons, using one of their elegant private suites as the backdrop. The goal was to create an intimate yet unforgettable evening, one where every detail felt custom-tailored to the guests. I wanted to elevate the experience with a touch of exclusivity, so naturally, I reached out to

Felicia Keith-Jones to help bring that vision to life. True to form, Felicia didn't just bring High Mark Distillery's award-winning spirits—she brought the heart of High Mark's philosophy: crafting experiences that leave a lasting impression.

Felicia arrived, not with a simple drink menu, but with an array of curated spirits and signature cocktails, each one carefully chosen to complement the atmosphere of the evening. Among the selections were High Mark's award-winning old fashioned, a cherry vanilla moonshine that felt like a nod to nostalgia with a modern twist, and a limoncello spirit so vibrant it seemed to bottle the very essence of summer. But what made this moment truly special wasn't just the spirits themselves; it was the way Felicia engaged with the guests. Rather than promoting High Mark as a brand, she focused entirely on creating an experience that made each person feel like they were part of something exclusive.

Felicia stood behind the bar, humbly serving drinks, but she wasn't just a mixologist for the night. She was part of the event, seamlessly blending into the conversations and connecting with guests on a personal level. She chatted with attendees about the spirits she crafted, not in a salesy way, but with a genuine warmth and enthusiasm that drew people in. As guests sipped their drinks, they didn't just taste a cocktail—they tasted the care, passion, and craftsmanship that went into each bottle.

True to the experience-first philosophy Felicia and I both believe in, we didn't name the drinks after High Mark. Instead, we named them after the event itself, creating a sense of exclusivity that made the guests feel like they were indulging in something crafted solely for that night, for them. This wasn't about High Mark's branding; it was about the people in the room. The spirits became part of the larger narrative of the evening, a complement to the experience rather than the focal point.

As the evening unfolded, it became clear that Felicia's presence had elevated the event to a whole new level. Guests didn't just feel like attendees; they felt like VIPs, sipping on custom-crafted cocktails while mingling in an atmosphere of warmth and exclusivity. It wasn't about luxury for luxury's sake—it was about making everyone in the room feel seen, appreciated, and part of something bigger.

This event was a perfect example of how Felicia and High Mark embody the true spirit of hospitality. It wasn't about showing off a product or pushing a brand; it was about connection. Each sip, each conversation, each shared moment contributed to the magic of the evening. That's the difference Felicia brings to every experience, and it's why her work—and her friendship—continue to play a pivotal role in everything we create together.

High Mark Distillery, under Felicia's leadership, is a company that understands one simple truth: branding isn't about plastering your name everywhere—it's about how you make people feel. It's about crafting moments that matter, about creating connections that last long after the bottle is empty. And that's the High Mark difference.

As our region expanded, this commitment to experience-first thinking became a critical part of our own growth strategy, a philosophy that would prove invaluable as we embarked on new ventures and reached new milestones.

After our class, Dr. Jaime Hope, Lindsay Smith, Felicia Keith-Jones and Cathy Christen behind the bar in the High Mark Distillery Tasting Room.

The Music and High Mark Distillery's
Signature Experiences

During the 2019 conference in Nashville, Felicia had one of her brilliant ideas. She suggested tapping into some of her musical connections to pull off a surprise country concert, stacked with Hall of Fame Singers and Grammy Winning Country stars and songwriters - Ken Peltier, Kendall Marvel, Bobby Tomberlin and Jimmy Webber. The band was set against the breathtaking backdrop of the Nashville skyline. It was one of those moments where you just know something magical is about to happen, and Felicia, as always, was speaking my language. We decided to keep the concert a secret from the rest of the attendees, adding an extra layer of excitement to an already electric evening.

The planning that went into it was nothing short of meticulous. Felicia worked her magic, organizing everything down to the finest detail. We carefully coordinated the arrival of the Country stars, discreetly setting them up for sound check while keeping everything hush-hush from the conference-goers. Every element—from the positioning of the stage to the timing with the caterers—had to be just right. It wasn't about putting on just another show; it was about curating an experience that would leave an impression long after the last note was played.

When the moment arrived, we gathered the group and made a casual announcement: it was time to change into something comfortable and meet us on the roof at an address we provided. Little did they know, a full-blown country concert with some of the best musicians in America awaited them. As we all ascended to the rooftop, the energy in the air was palpable. The city stretched out before us, bathed in the glow of the golden hour, and then the first chords strummed through the sound system. I'll never forget sitting up on the roof, slightly removed from the crowd, watching the women in attendance begin to beam with smiles, let loose and truly enjoy themselves. Laughter filled the air, the country music weaved into the Nashville night, and for that one magical moment, we were all connected in a shared experience that felt spontaneous, yet perfectly orchestrated.

The rooftop of our Nashville Country Concert with the incredible country talent that Felicia and I brought to life.

While we didn't have any of High Mark Distillery's spirits at the event, what we did have was something even more valuable—the essence of what High Mark stands for. The "High Mark spirit" wasn't just about a drink; it was about the feeling of being part of something larger than yourself, of creating a moment that would become a cherished memory. It was the same care and attention to detail that Felicia pours into every bottle at her distillery, but here, it manifested in a different form. It was about the people, the energy, and the unspoken sense of belonging that comes with an unforgettable experience.

The rooftop concert wasn't just an event; it was a reflection of what Felicia and I both hold dear in our work—the idea that when you focus on creating an experience, everything else falls into place. The music, the setting, the people—each element worked together to create a night that felt as personal as it was special. By the end of it, we weren't just conference attendees or colleagues; we were a part of something more, bound by the High Mark spirit that Felicia had woven into the fabric of the evening, even without a single branded bottle in sight.

In 2021, I was invited to attend a Tim McGraw concert in Reno, NV—a rare opportunity to enjoy a legendary performance up close. However, as serendipity would have it, the night before the concert, High Mark Distillery was hosting a special event featuring a live performance by country singer Ray Scott. The event was set at an outdoor Country Club pavilion in a picturesque community, where High Mark Distillery was asked to host the spirits. The location, with its open-air charm, immediately set the stage for an evening of energizing music, camaraderie, and exceptional drinks.

Upon arrival, I was greeted with a surprise: two other women from the very first women's group meeting I had attended years earlier were there too. In the warm Nevada evening, we caught up, sharing stories of where life had taken us since that fateful gathering. It was an unexpected reunion, a reminder of how connected our paths had become through these shared experiences. We grabbed seats together, letting Ray Scott's deep, soulful voice wash over us while sipping on custom-crafted cocktails made by High Mark. Each drink, whether a bourbon creation or a tangy whiskey concoction, was more than just a beverage—it was part of the evening's rhythm, seamlessly blending into the music and the ambiance.

What struck me was how naturally High Mark Distillery had become part of these moments. The spirits weren't the focal point, yet they enhanced the experience. Felicia's team, without pushing the brand, always found a way to weave High Mark into the backdrop, so it felt less like a sponsorship and more like an extension of the experience itself. The music, the drinks, the people—it all flowed together, creating a magical evening where High Mark was part of the narrative but never overshadowed the true star: the experience itself.

Fast forward to 2022. This time, I found myself invited to the birthplace of High Mark Distillery in Soldotna, Alaska, for another private concert, this one featuring Ken Peltier. Soldotna was a place rich with High Mark's roots, and you could feel the energy of that history the moment you stepped into the town. The setting for the concert was warm, intimate and rustic—family and friends gathered around, a food truck serving local bites, and a full bar stocked with High Mark Distillery's finest spirits. It wasn't flashy, but it was incredibly special, a curated evening brought to life by Felicia's vision.

Ken Peltier performed an acoustic set, and as his deep, rich, raw voice filled the Alaskan air, the experience took on a magical quality. The intimacy of the setting made it feel like he was playing just for us, for a small group of people lucky enough to share in this moment. The drinks, of course, were on point—whether you chose a neat whiskey or a cocktail crafted with one of High Mark's signature spirits, each sip complemented the warmth of the gathering. But again, what stood out wasn't just the taste of the spirits—it was the experience as a whole. The community felt closer, the evening felt more special, and each person in attendance felt like they belonged.

In Soldotna, Alaska at a private park hosted by High Mark Distillery, Ken Peltier and his fiddler performed for the crowd in an intimate setting.

The next day, after an early morning fishing excursion, I stopped by a local sandwich shop for lunch. As I sat down, I couldn't help but overhear a group of women in their mid-20s at the table next to me, excitedly chatting about "this incredible party" one of them had attended the night before. The party in question? None other than the private Ken Peltier concert. One of the women, who had been working the event as a cocktail server, was practically gushing about Felicia. She described Felicia as "the badass female distiller" who started in Alaska, and now ran one of the most talked-about distilleries in the region. The fact that even the staff at these events were left with such a strong impression speaks volumes. When an experience resonates not only with the guests but also with the people hired to serve, you know that something extraordinary took place.

This wasn't just another party. It was yet another moment where High Mark Distillery was seamlessly woven into the fabric of the evening. There were no branded mugs, no loud advertisements. Instead, there was an understated elegance, an atmosphere that made every person there feel special. High Mark had once again proven that it wasn't about being the loudest name in the room—it was about creating a space where the experience spoke for itself, where every guest felt like they were part of something unique, personal, and unforgettable.

In all instances—whether it was the concert in Nashville, or in Reno, or the intimate gathering in Soldotna—High Mark wasn't just a brand present at these events. It was an accompaniment to the deeper connections being made. It's this ability to seamlessly blend into the background, while still enhancing the experience for everyone involved, that sets High Mark apart. And it's what continues to inspire me as I reflect on the role of experiences in growing the West and beyond. The sense of connection and community built at these gatherings is a key lesson in how we approached every new challenge and opportunity that came our way during those crucial years of expansion.

Class is Now in Session

I had the opportunity to join one of High Mark's classes, open to the public, where Felicia taught everyone how to make a cocktail. In the room were about 20 individuals—small groups of 4 or so attendees knew each other, but the group was largely strangers. Over the course of the hour, the group became like a family—joined in the shared experience of making the cocktail.

Before we got started, each member of the group was able to sample the spirits that High Mark offered. We started with Apple Jack, then moved to Apple Jane, Vodka, Moonshine, and finally the Blueberry Cobbler Shine—which kind of felt like a dessert. Each was described to us along with the proper way to taste the spirits on our palates.

Master Distiller, Felicia Keith-Jones kicking off her cocktail making class with a history of High Mark Distillery and showcasing some of their spirits.

The drink we made was a cranberry drink mixed with vodka, tangerines, limes, cinnamon, and rosemary. What was so cool about the class was that it was an interactive but personal experience. Felicia explained what the different elements were meant to bring to the drink. And while I thought garnish was meant to make a drink pretty, it turns out each garnish is chosen to balance the flavors on your palate. Want a little more sweetness? Squeeze in the tangerine. Prefer a more tart flavor? Squeeze the lime. We were able to experience burning the cinnamon and the rosemary to bring those flavors into the drink and smell how it enhanced and incorporated itself into the experience. When we were finished, we mingled and sipped while nibbling on a cheese board and some chocolate candies. The Tasting Room was open, so we could visit the bar to taste the other spirits if we desired, and there was a cashier available should we want to purchase spirits to take home. The experience lasted for about an hour and was filled with so many memorable moments. If I lived closer, I'd be participating in every class they offer.

The cocktail that we made in class under Felicia's guidance and direction.

High Mark wasn't using this as a tactic to sell their spirits; they were offering the classes to showcase how their spirits could be incorporated into your life. The class I took was in October, and it was in preparation for the holiday season that was quickly approaching. How cool was it to have home bartenders able to create something worthy of being showcased at the most exclusive bar, right in their homes? I know I ordered a case of spirits to take home and to fill my liquor cabinet with—and to this day, High Mark is still the predominant label you'll see.

Whisked Away: Experiencing Alaska in a Whole New Way

Alaska had always been a dream of mine—a place that seemed wild, remote, and bursting with adventure. When my former company decided to open an office there, the stars aligned perfectly. I was about to merge business with pleasure in a way that I had always envisioned but never quite expected to unfold like it did. Coming from the East Coast, it made sense to turn this work trip into a longer getaway, but what I experienced was beyond anything I could have planned myself.

Naturally, the first person I reached out to for advice was Felicia Keith-Jones. Her connection to Alaska ran deep, having started High Mark Distillery there, and I knew she could point me in the right direction. What I hoped for was a list of places to visit, maybe some restaurants, or a local's insight into the best spots for tourists. What Felicia provided, though, was much more than a travel guide—it was an immersive experience that transformed Alaska from a destination into something far more personal. She didn't just offer me tips; she connected me with Jason Foster, the owner of Foster's Alaskan Cabins, a name that I'd come to associate with some of the most magical moments of my life.

Anyone who knows me, knows I am far from the "outdoorsy" type. Yet here I was, not only staying in an outdoor cabin in the rugged Alaskan wilderness, but also fully embracing the adventure. My first trip to Alaska wasn't just about work anymore; it became an opportunity to push my boundaries, and Jason made sure of that. He guided me into experiences that I never imagined for myself—like fishing for salmon on the Kenai River, eating our fresh catch right by the riverside, and later heading 65 miles off the coast of Seward for some halibut fishing. To this day, when I look back on that trip, it feels almost surreal—like stepping into another lifetime. These experiences weren't just activities to cross off a bucket list; they were connections made through Felicia's introduction and Jason's ability to craft moments that felt spontaneous yet deeply personal.

My business partner, Jim Campbell, and I fishing in Kenai, Alaska for fresh salmon.

One evening, Jason created something unforgettable—an impromptu gathering around a campfire by the river. Picture this: families and friends, bundled in sweatshirts to fend off the crisp Alaskan summer air, their cheeks tinged pink from both the chill and the flowing wine. A local man strummed a guitar, filling the night with music, while strangers-turned-friends sat around sharing stories, laughter, and warmth. It wasn't just a meal by the campfire; it was an experience, one of those rare moments where time seems to stretch, and you feel like you're part of something bigger than yourself. The air was filled with a kind of unspoken connection that only such an intimate, shared experience can create.

When my second trip to Alaska came around, there was no question in my mind where I would stay—I was returning to Foster's. This time, though, Jason had a few more surprises up his sleeve—as did Felicia. Upon landing in Kenai after a short puddle jumper from Anchorage, my business partner Jim and I were greeted by a woman dressed in a crisp white shirt and black pants. She knew our names immediately and told us Jason had sent her to pick us up. Little did I know, I was about to walk straight into a scene that felt straight out of a movie.

As we walked outside the tiny airport, I was scanning the parking lot for an Uber or a shuttle. But instead, what I saw was a white stretch limo parked right out front. I stood there clueless, still searching for my ride, when the driver stepped forward, opened the limo door, and invited us in. It was the ultimate "Pretty Woman" moment—a blend of surprise and delight that was so far beyond anything I could have expected. Inside the limo, Jason had thoughtfully stocked our favorite drinks, and what should have been a simple 15-minute ride to the cabins turned into an hour-long scenic tour of Kenai. By the time we pulled up to Foster's, guests were standing outside, curious to see who was arriving in such grand style. We weren't celebrities; we weren't VIPs; we were just two ordinary people. But Jason wanted us to feel like the experience was anything but ordinary.

And that's exactly the point. Jason doesn't just provide a place to stay; he curates an experience designed to make you feel special, like every moment is crafted with care. From riding horses on an Alaskan beach in Homer to a private Kenai River trout fishing tour, every day was filled with the kind of adventures that stay with you for a lifetime. We even had another day of halibut and rockfish catching off the coast of Seward. Jason's attention to detail and passion for creating memorable experiences were precisely why Felicia had insisted I stay there. He, like her, understands that it's not about the brand—it's about the people, the connections, and the memories made along the way. And waiting for us was none other than one of High Mark's famous spirits, a nod from Felicia to ensure Jason took extra good care of us—and that he did.

That's the magic of these experiences. They aren't scripted; they aren't branded—they're real, authentic moments that make you feel like you're part of something bigger. And those are the kinds of experiences that stay with you long after you've left Alaska.

The unforgettable experiences I had in Alaska serve as a perfect embodiment of the essence of High Mark Distillery, illustrating how the connections forged by Felicia transcend the mere presence of the brand. From the warm, welcoming atmosphere at Foster's Alaskan Cabins to the shared moments around the campfire, it was clear that the spirit of High Mark was alive and well, even in its absence. The kindness and attention to detail I experienced echoed Felicia's philosophy: it's about the people and the moments we create together, not just the products we offer. The relationships established through High Mark extend beyond distilling spirits; they forge a community that thrives on shared experiences and genuine connections. Whether it's a surprise concert overlooking the Nashville skyline or a cozy evening by the Kenai River, the High Mark experience lives on, woven into every gathering and interaction, reflecting the values that Felicia instills in her work. Even when High Mark isn't present, its influence can be felt in the heartfelt connections and the lasting memories that come to life through the people who believe in and embody its spirit.

FINDING A COMMON
THREAD

In reflecting on the success stories of Kimpton Hotels, Pieri Hospitality, and High Mark Distillery, a common thread emerges: each brand has mastered the art of creating memorable experiences that resonate deeply with their customers. Kimpton Hotels set the standard with its unwavering commitment to personalized service, offering unique touches that make every guest feel valued and appreciated. From their inviting lobbies to tailored guest experiences, Kimpton fosters an environment where connections are nurtured, ensuring that visitors leave with not just fond memories but a desire to return. This dedication to the guest experience has not only solidified their reputation but also transformed transient guests into loyal advocates.

Similarly, Pieri Hospitality thrives on the relationships it builds with its patrons. From the very beginning, the group has prioritized creating a sense of community within their venues. Their focus on curated experiences—from memorable events to personalized service—ensures that every visitor feels like part of the Pieri family. This approach extends beyond the dining experience; it encompasses every interaction, resulting in a loyal customer base that celebrates the brand's commitment to authenticity and connection. By cultivating an atmosphere where guests feel at home, Pieri Hospitality has succeeded in transforming diners into raving fans who share their positive experiences far and wide.

High Mark Distillery echoes this philosophy by placing significant emphasis on creating unforgettable moments that transcend the act of tasting spirits. Felicia Keith-Jones and her team prioritize the emotional connection formed with every visitor, whether through personalized distilling experiences or unforgettable events. They believe in the power of storytelling and connection, turning each encounter into a cherished memory. This customer-centric approach, coupled with a focus on community engagement and innovation, has allowed High Mark to create a loyal following that extends beyond the distillery's physical space. In each of these brands, we see how a commitment to exceptional experiences fosters genuine connections, ultimately leading to business growth driven by enthusiastic advocates who carry their stories into the world.

It's clear that the journeys of Kimpton Hotels, Pieri Hospitality, and High Mark Distillery illuminate a vital truth: it is not the brand itself but the exceptional customer experiences that fuel business growth and cultivate loyalty. By prioritizing meaningful connections and memorable interactions over mere branding, these companies have fostered a culture where customers feel valued, understood, and eager to return. This approach transcends traditional marketing tactics, transforming patrons into passionate advocates who share their experiences with others. Ultimately, it is this deep-rooted commitment to enriching customer experiences that serves as the cornerstone of sustainable growth, proving that in the ever-evolving marketplace, genuine relationships outshine logos and slogans. It is said that people do business with people they know, like, and trust—not that they do business with people who give them cool swag. And it is with this spirit that I was able to achieve extensive business growth as I launched a new region.

Section 2

Lessons from the Field—Building Experiences That Grow Businesses

Over the course of nine years as the Western region was growing, I realized firsthand how critical it was to focus on the experience we were providing to our customers. Sure, we had a product to sell, but what truly set us apart in a competitive market was the way we made our clients feel throughout every interaction.

In this section, I'll share with you some of the strategies and tactics we implemented that not only strengthened customer relationships but also helped us achieve significant growth. These aren't theoretical ideas—they're proven methods that worked for us and that can be adapted and applied to any business. From listening to customers' unspoken needs to creating personalized follow-ups, this section is packed with actionable insights that can help you foster deeper connections and grow your business. But first, let me tell you how I got started.

The Escalator Experience

After the Roaring 20s event in Phoenix, our next stop was Orlando, and I faced a unique challenge. Despite my best efforts, I couldn't find a venue that felt right. The bar had been set high in Phoenix—guests had been wowed by the experience at the Kimpton, and I knew that whatever we did in Orlando needed to exceed expectations. I wasn't just planning an event; I was curating an experience, one that would linger in people's memories long after the night ended.

That's when I connected with Hilarie of Café Tutu Tango, an eclectic, artistic space in the heart of Orlando. The restaurant itself was vibrant, but I needed something more—something that would transport our guests into another world. So I decided to transform the café and its adjacent parking lot into the lively streets of Havana. The event would be complete with a cigar roller, a fire dancer, a live band, roaming artists, and food that would be as unforgettable as the atmosphere. I had one goal: to create an experience that would captivate our guests from the moment they arrived.

As the tent for the event was being constructed, I made my way to the convention center to meet Jim. He was on his way to meet with a key prospect, Steve Chader, for the very first time. This was early 2015, and we hadn't signed any clients west of the Mississippi, something we ultimately decided to do because of Steve. Something instinctive stirred inside me as I saw Jim preparing to leave the booth and head down the escalator to the cafeteria, and I knew I had to go with him. It wasn't part of my original plan, but that didn't matter. It felt like a pivotal moment, though I wouldn't fully understand its significance until later.

At the time, I hadn't yet read Sheryl Sandberg's *Lean In*, but when I reflect on that day, it was my personal "lean in" moment. I made the decision to follow Jim down the escalator, quite literally and figuratively stepping into the opportunities that would soon shape the future of our company. That simple choice—following a gut instinct—opened doors I hadn't imagined.

When we arrived at the meeting with Steve, I sat down, unsure of how much I'd contribute. But as the conversation unfolded, it became clear that this was more than just a single business discussion. Steve had a vision for his company, and we were there to help bring it to life. We talked through possibilities, shared ideas, and found common ground. After the meeting, Jim and I went outside to debrief, and that's when I realized this was the beginning of something bigger.

That escalator ride wasn't just a ride—it was the start of a partnership, one where growing the Western region became a shared goal between Jim and me. It wasn't just about a job anymore; it was about passion and purpose, and I poured myself into it completely. I invited Steve to our Havana-themed event in Orlando that year, giving him his first taste of the VIP experience we were known for. It was more than just an invitation; it was an opportunity to show him who we were, what we could do, and the kind of personalized service we would deliver, time and time again.

From that night forward, Steve became more than a prospect; he became a raving fan, one of the first in the West to truly experience the magic of our VIP approach. The event not only solidified our relationship but also set the tone for every interaction we would have over the next nine years. Each experience we crafted built trust, each event deepened our connection, and each touchpoint strengthened his confidence in us. Steve became a crucial advocate for our brand, helping drive our expansion and contributing to the ultimate growth of the company.

Looking back on that escalator moment, I realize it wasn't just about leaning in—it was about stepping up, about recognizing that experiences are what fuel business growth. It's those deeply personalized, emotionally charged moments that transform clients into lifelong supporters.

This was only the beginning. As we continued to expand, the focus on creating unforgettable experiences became our secret weapon. With Steve's support and many others like him, the Western region would go on to thrive, each step forward guided by the same principles: connection, authenticity, and exceptional experiences.

Expanding into the West: More Than Just a New Office

The journey to establish a Western Division was a challenging yet defining chapter in our company's growth story and my own leadership development. As an East Coast-centered business, proposing a significant expansion to the West Coast required a lot of convincing. I spent countless hours analyzing market data, researching growth potential, and building a case around the tangible benefits of a physical presence in the region. It was crucial to demonstrate that the West was not only viable but also essential for achieving the next level of our company's growth and influence. This wasn't just about adding a new location for the sake of adding a new location; it was about securing our place in a competitive market, engaging with clients on their turf, and making a bold statement about our commitment to long-term growth.

Our CEO, Jim, was instrumental in championing this initiative within the boardroom. He had the experience, the drive, and the connections needed to make this vision feel achievable. I remember those initial boardroom meetings vividly—Jim relentlessly advocating for our strategy, supported by data we had prepared, and appealing to the Board of Directors' belief in the company's future. With his support, the board finally gave the green light, and we knew it was time to set big goals.

Once we had approval, I knew that my personal mission was to establish enough of a presence in the West to justify a permanent headquarters there. While working out of the Kimpton Living Room was an experience in and of itself, I envisioned this headquarters as a physical testament to our dedication to this market. A physical space would not only give our team a home base but would also solidify our presence for clients, employees, and the community.

This vision set a definitive target: to grow our operations with enough critical mass in the Western Division to warrant this new headquarters. I used to tell Jim that I wanted to plant our flags in Arizona so that everyone would be able to see them. And with a lot of teamwork, dedication, and strategic moves, we were able to reach that target in under four years. By 2019, we had achieved our Western Headquarters— a building that represented both our accomplishments and our ambitions. It was more than just an office; it was a symbol of all we had worked toward.

The day we opened the doors to our Western Headquarters was one of the most gratifying moments of my career. It was essential that this event reflect everything we had built—relationships, trust, and a culture of excellence. We wanted this opening to be a celebration of our journey, a gesture of gratitude to our partners and customers, and a clear signal of our commitment to the future.

Weeks before the event, we worked tirelessly to perfect every detail. I worked with a decorator to ensure that the office reflected our brand and the culture we wanted to foster in this new region. I recall spending hours working with her, choosing the decor, arranging furniture, and deciding how to create the perfect ambiance that would embody our values and vision. She hung two clocks on the wall, one set to Arizona time and the other to Pennsylvania time, symbolizing our new dual home bases. This wasn't just a design choice—it was a reminder of our company's journey from the East Coast to the West and of our shared identity. We built a training room large enough to seat 30 people, so that we could bring in classes and speakers to host meetings and expose visitors to who we were.

The two clocks in the office displaying Arizona and Philadelphia times.

To create a welcoming atmosphere, we paid careful attention to the amenities. The kitchen was thoughtfully stocked with coffee, tea, and other refreshments, embodying our hospitality-first philosophy. For the night of our Grand Opening, we also selected high-quality small bites and crafted cocktails for our guests to enjoy during the open house. And because we knew that little touches matter, we ensured each guest was greeted with their favorite beverage upon arrival—a gesture to show them they weren't just attendees but valued members of our journey.

At the Grand Opening of the Western Headquarters in the fully stocked kitchen, I stopped to take in the moment.

When the evening finally arrived, it was deeply fulfilling to see our vision come to life. Our partners, customers, and employees gathered to mark the occasion, many of whom had played critical roles in helping us reach this milestone. It was a moment of collective celebration and gratitude, a chance for everyone to connect and share in the story of our expansion.

I vividly remember watching the interactions that night. We had successfully brought together clients who, in any other context, would be considered competitors, yet here they were, united under our roof. They were meeting, laughing, and sharing stories with us and each other. It was an intimate, personal evening that went beyond a standard business event—it was a real moment of community. For me, it was a testament to everything we had accomplished up to that point and the relationships that had sustained our journey. Even today, when I close my eyes, I can still see the room that night and feel the energy within.

The Western Headquarters represented far more than just a new building. It symbolized our success in the region, our commitment to our customers, and our investment in building lasting relationships. The grand opening was a culmination of everything we'd worked toward: creating meaningful experiences, putting customers at the heart of our efforts, and building something that would stand the test of time.

The journey to get there was challenging, filled with difficult decisions, countless hours of hard work, and the proverbial blood, sweat, and tears—but it was worth every bit of effort. And it wasn't over. The building was our commitment made visible; it was a promise to our clients and the community that we were there to stay.

With the Western Headquarters established, we had a solid foundation for even more ambitious growth, though we didn't know the challenges the pandemic had in store for us. This milestone was only the beginning of what we wanted to achieve, as it now allowed us to operate from a place of stability and strength and gave us an added layer of confidence as we extended our footprint into other Western states. They would have a team of professionals based out of the Phoenix office who could serve them in addition to the headquarters in Pennsylvania. The West was no longer just a strategic target on a map—it was a real, thriving division with a dedicated home base, and the foundation we needed to pursue even greater objectives.

Make Them Feel Like VIPs

Inspired by the experiences that ignited my own journey at Kimpton, I knew that if we wanted our company to thrive, we needed to make every client feel like a VIP. This was a huge reason for our success and ultimately gave us the ability to open our Western Division headquarters. And the VIP journey started on Day 1.

Unlike other companies that relied on sales reps pounding the pavement, our business model took a different approach. Growth wasn't going to come from more people on the ground but from elevating the client experience from the start, creating something unforgettable and impactful that kept people coming back and engaged. That responsibility was on me and my business partner, Jim, and we knew that if we could create memorable experiences, growth would follow.

As business came in and clients joined us, we looked to scale in a way that would deepen relationships and make every interaction with us remarkable. One strategy we pursued was forming an exclusive partnership with Tony Giordano, a dynamic speaker who would deliver six sessions to clients, empowering them with strategies to grow their own businesses. But I didn't want these to be just seminars; I wanted to create a training experience that felt more like a private event. To do this, I chose to hold several of these events in the Kimpton Phoenix—a central location that aligned perfectly with the high-touch, experiential service we aimed to deliver.

The setup at Kimpton became a fusion of elegance and focus. Each event saw the ballroom transformed into an inspiring space with uplighting, custom florals, and a stage. Traditional classroom tables lined the room, but nothing else felt standard. Upon arrival, guests were greeted with handwritten notes, personally thanking them for joining us. Breaks weren't filled with boxed lunches or standard coffee; instead, guests enjoyed rich buffet spreads, from elaborate Asian cuisine to rustic Italian. It wasn't conference food; it was a culinary experience, down to the branded notebooks guests received to capture their learning moments. Each detail reflected the level of attention and care they could expect in their business dealings with us, showing them we weren't just another company but a partner who invested in excellence.

At the end of each seminar, we hosted a private dinner for around 20 select guests, creating an intimate mastermind experience with Tony. These gatherings weren't just meals; they were carefully curated events, where each guest received a personalized menu and a small booklet featuring everyone in attendance. Around the table, competitors sat together, not as rivals but as collaborators, sharing ideas and discussing strategies openly. This setting, far from a standard conference room, fostered trust, connection, and a sense of community—a space where they could genuinely engage and grow from one another.

The lesson was clear: by elevating a basic training session into a high-touch experience, we offered something beyond the typical seminar. We didn't give them merchandise; we gave them the skills to amplify their business tenfold, an invitation to a community, and access to industry peers in an environment that fostered real collaboration. This was more than branding; it was an immersive experience that stayed with them long after the event ended, offering real value and helping them feel part of something bigger.

One of the private master mind sessions held in the Kimpton Palomar Phoenix, complete with beautiful florals and custom menu cards.

When we hosted our second event, we planned an exclusive pre-seminar meeting where we invited clients to be featured and showcased on a panel of their peers. Plated lunches were served on white china, and we allowed our clients to have their moments to shine. They shared their knowledge with their peer group; they were the ones who were highlighted as experts, the ones people came to see. This personalized, exclusive touch rendered our panelists as subject matter experts—people their peers looked up to. It gave them a stage and a platform to showcase their accomplishments and to give the other attendees something to strive toward. We learned that while it was incredible to have professional speakers share knowledge, we had some hidden gems among our clients whom we could showcase as well.

Through these carefully designed experiences, we created raving fans. Clients weren't just loyal; they became ambassadors, spreading the word and bringing in more business. And as these relationships grew, so did our company. We learned that making people feel like VIPs—valuing them, investing in them, and creating experiences that went above and beyond—isn't just a nice gesture. It's the heart of sustainable business growth, and it's how we turned clients into lifelong advocates.

It's All About the Experience – and It Starts with the Team

In 2015, a business associate said something that completely shifted my perspective: "Lindsay, how can you expect your team to give Ritz-Carlton service when they've never been to the Ritz-Carlton?" That comment stuck with me. I was already invested in creating exceptional experiences for our clients, understanding how impactful a tailored, high-quality experience could be. But if we wanted to scale this belief, our team members needed to understand what premium service felt like firsthand.

I knew sending every team member to a luxury hotel wasn't realistic, but I could bring elements of that experience to them. I became focused on how to make every team interaction and event feel purposeful and customized, creating "Ritz-like" moments that resonated. Following my Kimpton experience, which set me into motion, I wanted our culture to feel like it was built around care and intention—not just for our clients but for our team members, too.

Our annual event in 2016 was my first chance to make this real. Rather than filling welcome bags with typical branded items, I wanted each gift to feel personal and thoughtful. Female team members received Kate Spade wristlets and Alex & Ani bracelets personalized with their initials, while male team members were given embossed wallets with theirs. This gesture went beyond gifting; it was the start of a mindset shift. These curated touches signaled to our team that this was the level of care we expected them to provide to clients.

In 2018, I introduced a new element to our events that went beyond professional training. I brought in speakers to help team members grow on a personal level, sharing the incredible resources and ideas I'd come across in my own career. This included experts in budgeting, vision boarding, conflict resolution, gratitude, stress management, and even manifesting one's life goals. I wanted them to experience what it felt like to have a company invest in them as individuals, helping them develop skills not just for work but for life.

That same year, we introduced a program encouraging team members to dedicate time to their communities. During a designated week each year, employees focused on community initiatives, whether it was a cause the company organized or a hyper-local effort they selected on their own. The sense of purpose it created was profound, extending the same care and respect we cultivated within the team outward into the community.

In 2019, we took another step in our commitment to team well-being, establishing an employee grant program for those facing hardships. Using a portion of the previous year's profits, we allocated funds based on a committee's review of monthly applications. This initiative allowed us to support employees through life's challenges, reinforcing a culture of care and support that transcended the workplace.

These efforts weren't just about cultivating loyalty or brand identity; they were about setting a tone of genuine care and investment in our people's lives. This belief wasn't just something we applied to customers; it was a cornerstone of our company culture. By elevating the employee experience, we didn't just enhance our service standards—we created advocates within our team who brought that same attention, thoughtfulness, and purpose to their clients. We learned that extraordinary service wasn't an external objective; it was an internal practice that, when cultivated in the team, would naturally overflow into the client experience. And this, in turn, became the catalyst for our company's growth and success.

We personalized attendee gifts with their initials and a hand written note card addressed to them. The bags were filled with more personalized gifts celebrating them.

The COVID Crisis

It's safe to say that the year 2020 brought massive emotions to everyone. I remember sitting in our boardroom in March, forecasting out the year and testing to see how long we could operate with zero revenue due to the shutdown. While we had two or three months where things were slower than we were accustomed to, no one could have predicted the massive spike in business that we would receive. With additional restrictions on businesses and groups, our team members were doing twice the work on each transaction. A traditionally busy summer became one of unsurpassed business highs. We knew we needed to do something to keep our teams focused on the experience, so we decided to invest in creating "experiences in a box" for our team members to enjoy at home with their families, understanding that their families were critical to their, and our, ultimate success.

And so it was born. In the fall of 2020, we hand-built custom experience boxes specific to each family and delivered them to their homes. We started with a custom S'mores Kit—complete with gourmet marshmallows, enough metal s'more skewers for the family, and a recipe book with new takes on s'mores.

That December, we sent a box filled with Otterbox **mugs** with each family member's initials on them, gourmet hot chocolate, pancake mix—and as the demand for some "Cool Company Swag" arose, we included T-shirts for each family member.

In February, we sent custom pizza kits complete with pizza sauce, a dough recipe and all of the ingredients, a pizza stone, and a dish towel—

all customized with a quote on them. In May, we celebrated Cinco De Mayo with a Taco Tuesday box—featuring taco stands for everyone in the family, a chip and dip set with the family's last initial on it, salsa from one of the states we had opened in, infused margarita mixes, and some fun maracas. That August, we sent a summer gift of a luau kit—complete with beach towels embroidered with each family member's initials, tropical drink mixes, recipes, and games for them to host a luau, along with leis and flower hair clips. The boxes were meant to be fun and a nod to the team members' lives outside of the office.

The contents of the Cinco de Mayo boxes included a taco cookbook, a personalized chip and dip, special seasonings, tac holders, a drink infuser, baby maracas and tequila.

These experiences helped to build a strong internal culture, which naturally translated to better customer service. Our team felt valued, and they passed that feeling on to our clients. Creating personalized experiences doesn't just delight—it builds brand loyalty and elevates your service.

Translation to Our Clients

The success of our personalized "family boxes" approach inspired us to rethink how we could create memorable, impactful gestures for clients to close out their transactions with us. We realized that while a standard "thank you" was expected, what clients rarely received was an authentic, thoughtful gift that celebrated their personal journey with us. So, each office took the core concept of a personalized thank-you gift and added their own unique spin to make it feel relevant to both the client and the team involved.

Some offices chose to gift pencil sketches of the homes their clients had just bought or sold, giving them a beautiful keepsake of a place tied to personal memories and major milestones. Others put together personalized cutting boards, blending practicality with sentiment—a gift the clients could use in their new kitchens and think of fondly for years to come. In a more utilitarian approach, some teams put together "Welcome Home" baskets filled with essentials like paper towels, snacks, and other necessities to make those first few nights in a new space as stress-free as possible.

This approach gave each team the freedom to add their personality to the gesture. The results were not only unique but truly resonated with clients. Without a branded touch, these gifts shifted the focus to the client and celebrated their journey, which ultimately deepened their connection to our company. And in the process, we created more than just customers; we built advocates who would continue to share our story with others, driving growth organically.

Elevating the Onboarding Experience

As we grew, the need for team members grew. I saw an opportunity to enhance the onboarding experience for new team members. We were seeing a high rate of turnover and struggling to find culturally aligned talent who believed in our mission. After working with a recruiter, I identified a gap in the way we were bringing people onboard and created a pilot program to follow employees from the moment they said yes—even before they stepped into the company—through their first six months of employment.

It started with a series of emails that showcased who we were as a company and highlighted some of the things that made us uniquely us. So that an employee wasn't walking in and hearing words, terms, and phrases they didn't understand, we taught them. We shared our Core Values, the meaning behind our annual events, and some of the things that we, as an organization, were committed to.

Before they stepped foot into their office, they received a backpack with some company swag at their house. This was meant to help them feel like they were already a part of the company. On Day 1, they received a box with all the things they might need for their new space, a training manual, a copy of Jon Gordon's *The Energy Bus,* and flowers from Farm Girl Flowers. They were assigned an Employee Experience Manager who would check in with them, ensure they met each department, and guide them through the training process.

One of the elements we created was a "Meet the C-Suite," where each week, all new employees met via Zoom with the Executive Team of the company. It was an opportunity for team members to ask questions, see the leadership team, and feel connected. Each member of the team shared their journey as well as something personal about themselves, helping to foster connection. New hires were given direct contact information and offered the opportunity to ask questions directly and to share who they were—as a human being, not just as an employee. These thirty-minute sessions were massively impactful in making team members feel welcomed and special. Time after time we'd hear, "I've never talked to a CEO before"—and every time it made me smile. The availability of our Executive Team was something I was incredibly proud of and something that set us apart.

Another part of the onboarding required the Employee Experience Specialist to check in weekly with the new hires and go over some thought-provoking questions about *The Energy Bus.* You see, our first core value was "Embrace Positivity," and we believed that if we could focus on that positivity and its impact from Day 1, our teams would be best set up for success both in life and in our organization.

Ultimately, we transitioned from a Human Resources Department to a People Operations Department, focusing on the needs of our employees and the understanding that they were human beings first and foremost. This shift encouraged people to open up and have conversations that they would have felt intimidated to have with a traditional Human Resources Team. Our team became employee advocates who balanced the employees' needs with the organization's expectations.

Interactive Partner Meetings

We didn't just have meetings with our employees; we held quarterly meetings with our partners. Traditionally, like most business reviews, these meetings were structured around straightforward data points—profit and loss, projections, and performance assessments. But as we developed the new region, it became clear that these meetings could be a lot more than a corporate formality. In one of our partnerships in Florida, launched concurrently with the Western Division, the idea surfaced to make these gatherings both interactive and transformative, to foster genuine collaboration and create an open environment for all partners to share insights and ideas. This was more than just an opportunity to present numbers; it was a chance to build our business together from the ground up.

In 2018, after earning my certification as an Xchange Facilitator, I began integrating facilitation techniques to foster open dialogue, creativity, and joint problem-solving. The traditional thirty-minute meetings expanded into in-depth, three-hour sessions, structured around active participation. The goal was simple but powerful: bring everyone's ideas to the table and allow partners to have a genuine voice in the decisions and directions that would shape the business. We introduced activities that allowed partners to not only hear but also respond to one another's ideas, fueling a more engaged, collaborative energy. Each partner meeting started with a "wisdom of the crowd" session, where everyone shared their thoughts on recent challenges, opportunities, and service improvement ideas— and in some sessions, I pulled out their inner child by giving them arts and craft supplies, asking them to create.

The immediate impact was profound. Partners began contributing valuable ideas that reshaped our service levels, introduced innovative concepts, and created unique service standards. They didn't just talk about best practices—they defined and refined them in real time. We took the ideas generated in these sessions and brought them back to the team with newfound enthusiasm and clarity. The ownership they felt created a ripple effect, translating into higher engagement in the offices and a heightened sense of accountability to uphold the standards they'd had a hand in setting. These sessions ultimately fueled year-over-year growth and continuous improvement, with partners and their teams bringing a shared vision to life.

As we wrapped up each partner meeting, we didn't simply disperse and move on with our days. Instead, we concluded with an informal social gathering—a relaxed cocktail hour where the formality of the boardroom gave way to a more personal environment. It was here that we deepened the bonds we'd begun to build in the formal meeting, connecting over life updates, shared stories, and laughter. These informal gatherings were as important as the structured meetings, creating a network of trust and camaraderie that transcended business interests. Partners shared their personal journeys, and friendships formed that would support them in business and beyond.

By 2024, the impact of these quarterly gatherings was undeniable. We had cultivated a team of partners who were more than colleagues—they were committed advocates for the brand and for one another's success. They were motivated by a shared sense of purpose and inspired by the direct impact they were making on the business's direction and future.

When the time came for my own farewell, it was this same group of partners who sent me off with heartfelt words and an overwhelming sense of appreciation. Their genuine messages and reflections on our time together underscored what I had always hoped to achieve—a culture of connection, collaboration, and collective ownership.

These partner meetings had evolved from routine updates into a driving force for our business's growth and a vital part of our corporate culture. Together, we had built a foundation of mutual respect, shared vision, and camaraderie, proving that when everyone feels like a valued contributor, the whole team rises.

Social Media Clues

Social media often gets a bad rap for being a time-waster, a distraction from reality. But it's also an incredibly powerful tool for deepening relationships—especially in business. I discovered this early on and dedicated time to mastering it, later sharing these insights with my team to strengthen connections with clients.

I saw this firsthand with Travis at Kimpton. He had researched my LinkedIn profile to ensure that the staff would recognize me by name when I arrived, embodying Dale Carnegie's principle that "a person's name is to that person the sweetest and most important sound in any language." Being recognized instantly and greeted by name sealed the deal for me and made me feel like a VIP from the start. This wasn't simply an event at a beautiful venue; it was the beginning of a personalized experience that connected me to the brand on a deeper level. Social media had allowed him to know me just enough to make that personal connection, which instantly made my experience feel unique.

Tony Giordano, who spoke at one of our seminars, shared how social media could act as a superpower, offering insight into clients' lives, interests, and values. These platforms are rich with clues about a person's milestones, family dynamics, and personal values, giving businesses an opportunity to build authentic connections. Social media done well isn't a sales tool—it's a tool for understanding people and finding real ways to relate.

Social media cues also provide the ability to "surprise and delight" in unforgettable ways. For example, on my tenth wedding anniversary, I received an incredible surprise from a client: a replica of my wedding bouquet. We had never spoken about my anniversary, let alone my wedding flowers, and I certainly hadn't provided any of that information myself. But he had taken the time to look at my Facebook page, finding and using those details to create a gift that was profoundly personal. As he later shared with me, he had a team member dedicated to reviewing social accounts to identify "surprise-worthy" moments. That little bit of insight allowed him to create something that went far beyond a typical client gesture. His thoughtfulness left a lasting impression on me, something I would carry for years and share with others.

The flowers I was gifted by a client for my 10th Wedding Anniversary, complete with picasso calla lilies, like my wedding bouquet.

It's not only major gifts that leave an impact; it's the intentionality behind even the smallest gestures. That same client shared how he once received two beach buckets filled with shovels and sand toys for his kids before a family vacation. It was a small, simple gift, but it resonated deeply. Those buckets might have been inexpensive, but the gesture was priceless because it said, "We see you; we know what's important to you." He used this approach in his own real estate business in California, surprising clients with thoughtful, timely gestures that turned standard interactions into memorable experiences. I don't need to buy a home in California, but I can tell you that if I ever do, I know who I would buy from—and it's because he's made a habit of listening and responding in ways that make his clients feel valued beyond the transaction.

It's these small, meaningful gestures—remembering someone's name, marking their milestones, or acknowledging life events—that transcend the typical customer-business relationship. These moments become etched into our memories and build lasting loyalty, creating raving fans without ever needing to push a brand. When done right, social media isn't about branding at all; it's about human connection. And those connections, as small as they may seem, are what make a business grow.

Connecting Through Conversations

Sometimes, cues come in person. I was at a meeting with a client and a potential client in Las Vegas. We had a wonderful conversation about travel, vacations, and memories. We got on the topic of luggage, and one guest, let's call him Jack, said he had watched his luggage leave the airport after a recent trip to Nepal, tracking it using the AirTag he had placed inside. He shared about the numerous vaccines one needed to receive before traveling there—something like ten shots he had gotten in preparation for the trip. Jack also shared his desire to go to Mount Kilimanjaro and hoped to go that summer.

Another guest, let's call her Lauren, mentioned that when she visited France years ago, she had a black suitcase with pink polka dots. When she got home, she opened the luggage to find it filled with diapers! Clearly, this was before the age of AirTags. A quick look at the name on the luggage tag revealed she had picked up the wrong luggage. She later met up with the person she had inadvertently switched with and exchanged bags.

I was genuinely engaged in the dinner conversation and felt like we had all connected over the meal, so I wanted to thank them both for spending their time with me. When I got back, I sent Lauren a bottle of French wine and a black tote bag with pink polka dots, along with a note that read something like, "I hope this brings back French memories for you."

As for Jack, I found two books on Mt. Kilimanjaro, a T-shirt that said, "I'm vaccinated," and a list of all the vaccines needed for entry into Tanzania. Months later, Jack reached out to me. He said he had almost decided not to book the trip, but seeing the book on his shelf reminded him of his dream, and he knew he had to go. He thanked me for being the catalyst that pushed him to say "yes" to this epic experience.

Neither gift cost a fortune; in fact, both were under $50. However, the impact of those gifts on a personal level deepened their relationships with me and with the brand I represented. Lauren went on to become a client, and Jack continued to support the business. I could have easily sent them a branded mug and a note saying, "I hope we can do business together," but I didn't. Instead, I chose to make the follow-up something that took effort, showed I had listened to them, and connected to something meaningful to them. Personalization doesn't mean showering someone in lavish gifts; it means listening and finding something uniquely suited for that person. Had I sent those two gifts to any other two people, they wouldn't have had any meaning—but for Jack and Lauren, they were deeply personal.

This experience reinforced the idea that personalization doesn't have to be expensive; it just needs to show attentiveness and care.

Cultivating Relationships—Acknowledging Times of Sympathy

Sometimes, experiences come when you least expect them, from gestures that are genuine. An out-of-state business partner's father passed away. Searching for something meaningful to send, I ordered a custom wind chime with his father's name on it and had it delivered to his house. He thanked me for the gift, and I didn't think much about it after that because, truly, it was a sincere gesture, not a business tactic.

About nine months later, the same business partner reached out to let me know he'd been thinking of me. He shared that each night he takes a walk and returns home to the wind chime hanging on his front door. He said he always thought he would remember his dad after his passing but never imagined he could develop a kind of relationship with him in the afterlife. However, the gift of the wind chime allowed him to do so. Every evening after his walk, he gently moves the wind chime, and as it plays, he looks up at the sky and talks to his dad. He never imagined that thinking of and talking to his dad every day would be possible—but with that gift, it was.

Was the gift meant to connect him to his dad? Certainly not. It was simply a token of my sympathy during his time of need. Yet, that gift led him to create a nightly ritual and experience honoring his father, bringing him peace. Notably, my name isn't on the wind chime, nor is my company's logo. It's uniquely his, with his father's name on it. But every night, as he thinks of his father, he also remembers me and the company I was with when I gave it to him.

This deeply personal experience not only reinforced our professional relationship but also led to him advocating for our company with other business partners. The impact of the wind chime wasn't about brand visibility—it was about genuine human connection. And because of that, it became a touchstone in our relationship.

The Power of Connection—Face-to-Face Experiences

Face-to-face presence is powerful, and it became a cornerstone of our success despite the 2,500 miles separating our headquarters from the growth region. Between one and two weeks each month were spent traveling, connecting directly with clients, partners, and team members, strengthening relationships and reinforcing our brand's commitment and culture. I believe that consistent in-person leadership was instrumental in driving success, but there were a couple of instances that truly underscored the impact of being there, in person, at critical junctures.

One of those instances happened early in our division's launch. We discovered that the infrastructure we'd put in place wasn't sustainable. The day before we were set to fly home, we had to make some tough decisions, rework processes, and communicate new plans—decisions that impacted everyone. While it would have been easier to hop on that plane and follow up with an email laying out the changes, we knew that wouldn't match the experience we were building. So, we extended our stay, arranged an in-person meeting, and invited team members to our largest office to share what had happened and explain our plan to move forward. We spoke candidly and with vulnerability, explaining not only the challenges we'd encountered but also our commitment to support them as they adjusted to the new direction. I assured them that I'd manage their needs from afar, taking phone calls, troubleshooting issues, and staying connected to help them navigate the coming months. This commitment stretched from June to December of 2016, during which I worked remotely until we could appoint an on-site leader.

The second pivotal moment came when issues arose in a specific office. On a Friday, we received word of the challenges, and by Monday morning, we were in Arizona, meeting the team in person. Sharing a meal and discussing issues over lunch helped resolve immediate concerns, but it did more than that. Showing up on such short notice demonstrated our dedication to the partnership, solidified our relationships, and showed our team members they were worth every mile of travel.

I know neither I nor the company was perfect. But the act of showing up in person—especially during challenges—demonstrated a dedication to the people on our team. It wasn't about merely solving problems; it was about sitting across from someone, making eye contact, and showing that we were there not just in good times but also when things got tough. We listened, empathized, and collaborated in real time. It was an approach that consistently reinforced our message that we were partners, not just in business but in the experience and journey we were creating together.

From Large, Elaborate Events to Intimate Dinners

Creating memorable dining experiences isn't just about where you go or even what you eat; it's about the details that turn an otherwise ordinary meal into something unforgettable. It's easy to book a table at a nice restaurant, but crafting an experience is another level entirely. The space, the setup, and the thoughtfulness woven into every aspect transform it from "just a dinner" into an event that sticks in your memory. Unless you're dining somewhere naturally unique—perhaps a restaurant with a month-long waiting list or one that offers world-renowned cuisine— creating a standout experience often falls on the host's shoulders. Over the years, I've learned the power of taking control of those details.

Every time I planned a dinner, particularly for larger groups or special occasions, custom menu cards became a must. These details give an event a special flair and make guests feel like VIPs, seeing something designed just for them. It's surprisingly easy to do—tools like Canva have endless templates to fit any mood or theme. With some creativity and personalization, these small gestures become powerful. Adding each person's name to the menu, designing a logo or motif, or highlighting specialty cocktails made just for the night were small touches that could create an impression.

One of our most memorable events happened in 2015 at a massive real estate conference in Orlando, where we crafted the "Havana Nights" experience. It set a high bar for future events, complete with tropical decor, custom cocktails, and an atmosphere that made our attendees feel like they'd stepped into a Cuban paradise. Inspired by that success, we pushed the envelope even further in 2016 in New Orleans, transforming an old airplane hangar into a scene right out of *Moulin Rouge*. The night was complete with live silk performers, a VIP area, a live band, and traditional Creole cuisine. Every detail was intentional, from the costumes of the performers to the decor, which transformed the space into an extravagant ballroom. Before the event began, we organized an intimate Q&A with expert speakers so that guests left with both unforgettable memories and valuable business insights.

Jim and I at the Moulin Rouge Event in New Orleans.

After those larger events, though, we noticed a challenge: while these events attracted hundreds, it was tough to connect meaningfully with all 800 guests. By 2017, we pivoted to focus on more intimate gatherings, beginning with an event in Las Vegas where we reserved a section at the Four Seasons. This was different—it wasn't about the grand scale but the one-on-one connections. We brought in a roaming magician and a guitarist to entertain, creating an atmosphere that fostered conversation.

Our group of about 100 guests allowed us to engage with each person, a welcome shift from the massive events. It felt like we could finally give our full attention to each guest, deepening relationships and making each individual feel genuinely appreciated.

As our approach to events evolved, we began organizing even smaller dinners, usually with around 20 attendees. These events allowed for intimate conversations and genuine connections. With fewer people, the personalization could shine. For each dinner, I made sure everyone had a customized menu and a small, thoughtful gift—usually something personal like a leather wallet embossed with their initials. And handwritten notes became an absolute staple. I wrote thousands of notes over the years, but to this day, I wouldn't have done it any differently. Those notes represented our commitment to making each guest feel seen, valued, and remembered.

Steve Chader, Lindsay Smith, Jennice Doty and Jim Campbell join together at an event in Las Vegas at the Four Seasons. Steve and his business partner Jennice were crucial to our success in the west and became dear friends to both Jim and myself.

The last major event before COVID holds a special place in my memory. We hosted it at a stunning glass-enclosed steakhouse in Dallas. The tables were decorated with lush custom flowers, and each guest's place setting featured a beautifully wrapped box containing a personalized, embossed leather good, tied with a blue ribbon and sealed with their name. There was something magical about that evening. As I mingled with our clients, sharing laughs and expressions of gratitude, I felt connected to each person in the room. I even gave a short speech to acknowledge everyone's contribution to our collective success. The smaller scale allowed me to float from table to table, engaging in meaningful conversations that made everyone feel included.

These events became a sort of trademark for our brand. When clients received an invitation to a dinner or an event with us, they anticipated more than just a meal. They knew they were in for a unique experience, whether it involved a champagne toast on a rooftop overlooking the Vegas Strip, an evening at a long table in the midst of a vibrant drag show in Orlando, or a secluded dinner in a private wine cellar in New Orleans. Each gathering was thoughtfully crafted to provide a little extra magic, an "icing on the cake" moment that complemented the relationships we'd built.

In creating these experiences, we cultivated a culture that transcended ordinary business interactions. Our goal wasn't just to entertain; it was to build relationships, nurture trust, and leave a lasting impression. These experiences turned clients into friends and acquaintances into lifelong contacts. This approach to hospitality reflected a deeper philosophy: that genuine connections, supported by thoughtful details, set the foundation for lasting success.

Legacy of Growth

Looking back, I feel filled with gratitude and pride—not only for what we achieved but for how we achieved it. The nine years I spent shaping the growth of our Western Region showed me that customer loyalty isn't won through clever marketing alone or momentary perks. It isn't about a discount or a sale. It's earned through genuine, thoughtful experiences that consistently reinforce the trust customers place in you. The bonds created and nurtured through meaningful interactions became a testament to how deeply a brand can impact someone's life.

These experiences gave me a firsthand understanding of why loyalty grows out of more than just excellent service; it grows from creating something truly unforgettable for each person who crosses your path. And that's the lesson I carry forward: when we approach every touchpoint with purpose and authenticity, we invite customers, partners, and team members to stay—not because they have to, but because they genuinely want to.

Section 3

How Do You Surprise and Delight?

10 Real-Life Examples of Integrating Surprise and Delight into Business

In business, the art of surprising and delighting customers must be rooted in authenticity to have a real impact. While you can implement systems to consistently surprise and delight, each instance must feel personal and tailored to the individual. It's not just about following a formula; it's about creating genuine moments that resonate. And while the idea of surprising and delighting customers might seem overwhelming or even costly, it doesn't need to break the bank. It's all about paying attention to the little things that matter and showing your customers that they are truly valued.

In this section, I'll provide ten simple yet powerful ideas that you can start implementing right away. These ideas will help you elevate your customer experience and, in turn, drive your business forward. Whether it's a thoughtful gesture, a personalized follow-up, or a small surprise that exceeds expectations, each of these tactics is designed to deepen relationships and grow your market share. With a little creativity and intention, you can make your clients feel seen, heard, and appreciated in ways that leave a lasting impact.

For me, these thoughtful gestures not only deepened relationships but also led to significant growth in our company's market share.

Surprise & Delight Secret #1:

Remember Customer Preferences

To surprise and delight effectively, you need to collect and organize key details about your customers. To do so, I recommend a customer profile sheet. It doesn't need to be fancy—just something to collect information about your customers or prospects so that you have it at hand. I use a simple customer profile sheet to track personal information like birthdays, favorite travel destinations, and family milestones. Kimpton, for instance, has a lengthy customer profile that customers can fill out online if they want to do so. The Notes app on your phone, an Excel document, or an old-fashioned notebook all work just fine. Whether you use a spreadsheet, a notes app, or a CRM tool, having this information readily available can help you create moments of surprise that are deeply personal. On my website, www.amplify-experiences.com, you'll find a downloadable template that you can use. You'll want the ability to change, add, and delete items. Many of these questions can be filled out through a little social media exploration.

For example, whenever I stay at a Kimpton property, they greet me by name, send a bottle of wine to my room, and often upgrade my reservation—all based on details I've provided in their customer profile system. These gestures, repeated across multiple stays, make me feel valued and understood, which has turned me into a loyal customer. I've even planned vacations around staying at Kimpton properties because of the consistently personalized experience.

This same principle can be applied to any business. Keep track of your regular customers' preferences and surprise them with a personalized touch, like greeting them by name, knowing their usual order, or setting up their favorite service options in advance. This attention to detail not only surprises customers but also makes them feel truly valued and understood.

When you know your clients well, it's easier to surprise and delight them in ways that matter.

Surprise & Delight Secret #2:

Not Your Ordinary Trade Show or Conference

How many trade shows have you attended where guests walk away with bags full of swag? How many of those bags end up in the trash or left in the hotel room? Trade shows are notorious for the piles of branded swag that attendees collect and often discard. But instead of investing in pens and mugs, why not create an experience that attendees will remember? I believe that if someone studied a trade show attendee and participant, they'd find the same thing—neither are connected to the swag, and the swag doesn't convert to a relationship. What if, instead of spending $500 on pens and mugs, a vendor spent $500 to offer something an attendee would actually use?

What if vendors had a selection of flip-flops for the ladies who were adamant about wearing heels until they'd finished their 10th mile in the convention center? What if vendors offered an infused water station to combat the jugs of water or the lines at the concession stands? Or still, if a vendor made fresh cookies or popped fresh popcorn? Or what if a vendor offered an interactive station where an attendee could blow off some steam or shake the stress from their shoulders by playing a virtual reality game or punching a punching bag? All of these ideas are simple and relatively cost-effective. None of them include a branded item. All of them allow for genuine conversation and for a memorable moment to happen at the convention, and—assuming you target the right people— could lead to increasing your client base.

Years ago, I was a vendor at a conference in San Diego, and we hosted a Wii Tournament where attendees could try their hand at bowling. We were a favorite booth—and because of the activity, we had more than 10 seconds to speak to clients and prospective clients, which gave us more intel to use in our follow-up.

This approach helped us stand out, leading to more meaningful follow-ups and, ultimately, more conversions. A memorable experience sticks with people far longer than generic swag ever could.

Surprise & Delight Secret #3:

Turning Feedback into Action

I was at a seminar this past spring in Napa. Days were filled with meetings and dinners—and both nights of the conference, a bottle of wine was delivered to my room. With only carry-on luggage, I couldn't bring the wine home, and I hardly had time to drink it while I was there. A well-intended gesture fell flat. An opportunity for them to shine was in the meeting room—and they missed the mark. The room was freezing. It was a small group of people, under 50, and everyone was complaining about the cold during the meeting, the break, and upon returning. The planner missed a huge opportunity. She saw everyone, she heard everyone, and she stood there. What if she had used the feedback and gone to the store across the street to buy a handful of pashminas? I know this was possible because after the session, I went and purchased two—for $16 each. I'm confident that $16 was cheaper than the bottles of wine—and the impact would have been huge. A simple, "Hey, I noticed the room was cold—would you like to choose a pashmina from this basket?" The wine was a gift. The pashmina would have been an experience.

If you listen to your customers in the moment and act accordingly, you can transform a negative situation into an opportunity to surprise and delight.

Surprise & Delight Secret #4:
Personalized Follow-Ups

After one memorable meeting with a prospect, I decided to follow up with a small gesture of appreciation. I sent a handwritten thank-you note, but I didn't stop there. During our meeting, the prospect had casually mentioned a book on his reading list that he hadn't yet picked up. I jotted the title down in my notes, thinking it might come in handy. When I mailed the thank-you note, I included a copy of that book. This wasn't a grandiose gift, nor was it an extravagant expense. But it was personal, tailored to his interests, and showed that I had been listening to what mattered to him.

The power of personalized follow-up is its ability to convey genuine thoughtfulness and attention to detail. That gesture with the book did more than express my gratitude—it showed that I cared enough to make the effort to learn about his interests and remember them beyond our meeting. In a world where transactions often feel impersonal, this small act stood out. The prospect later told me that he was both surprised and impressed by my gesture, and it was clear that this thoughtful follow-up helped tip the scales in my favor when it came to closing the deal.

Personalized follow-ups work because they communicate more than just words on a page; they convey respect, attentiveness, and a willingness to go beyond the basics. Too often, follow-up efforts are generic, making them easy to ignore or forget. How often have we all received the same tired, template-based email after a meeting or phone call? An effective follow-up breaks away from this predictability and does something unexpected. It turns an otherwise transactional exchange into a relationship-building opportunity.

There are many ways to approach personalized follow-ups. For example, consider sending a handwritten note that references specific points from your conversation. Mentioning something unique about the meeting—whether it was a shared laugh, a surprising connection, or a topic they're passionate about—shows that you've put thought into the message. Even just taking the time to handwrite a note in today's digital age can leave a lasting impact.

In some cases, a personalized follow-up could include sending an article, podcast, or video link relevant to a topic discussed. In a recent conversation with someone who was looking to hire a COO, he shared that he didn't have the job description written out. I followed up with a copy of Cameron Herald's *The Second in Command* with a note that said, "I hope this helps you finalize your job description." Needless to say, the gentleman reached out to let me know he received the book, and then again after he'd read it.

Let's say a client mentions their interest in traveling abroad or learning about how high performers set themselves up for success. Following up with an insightful article on those subjects, along with a brief note on why you thought it would resonate with them, shows that you care about their interests beyond the scope of your business interaction. When you take the time to connect with someone on a personal level like this, it positions you not just as a service provider but as a resource and a thoughtful contact.

In another instance, I was meeting with a potential client who mentioned how he and his sons loved trying new bottles of scotch. I found a site that allowed for customization of the bottle and sent it to him with a note to enjoy with his son. The cost was relatively minor, but the gesture paid dividends in relationship-building. When he received the bottle, he reached out not only to thank me but to express his appreciation for the thoughtfulness of my follow-up. This simple gesture solidified our relationship, making our future interactions more comfortable and ultimately helping secure his business. Small gestures like these illustrate that you're not simply in it for a sale; you're looking to create a memorable experience.

Of course, personalized follow-ups don't always have to involve physical items. Sometimes, it can be as simple as making a quick call or sending a note to check in, particularly if the person mentioned a life event or personal milestone. For example, following up after someone mentions their child's graduation or a recent trip with a quick message to ask how it went shows that you're not just keeping tabs on them as a client but are genuinely interested in them as a person.

The real power in personalized follow-ups is that they don't need to be expensive or extravagant; they just need to be genuine. Too often, we overthink these efforts, feeling that they need to be grand gestures to make an impact. But more often than not, what matters is simply that you took the time to listen and respond meaningfully. When you make people feel seen, valued, and respected, they're more likely to think highly of you and consider your business offerings favorably. In an increasingly automated world, this human touch goes a long way.

In my experience, clients often remember these small acts of thoughtfulness long after the fact. They may not always mention it directly, but they notice it, and it has a compounding effect on their loyalty. This effect is especially noticeable when it's contrasted with the typical business follow-up, which can feel robotic and indifferent. By showing you're willing to put in a little extra effort, you stand out in a competitive landscape. It's not just about what you sell or the services you provide; it's about how you make people feel in every interaction.

The impact of personalized follow-up extends beyond individual transactions, too. It builds a reputation of thoughtfulness and reliability, reinforcing a brand image that prioritizes people over profit. Clients who feel cared for are more likely to share positive experiences with others, which can lead to valuable word-of-mouth referrals and lasting business relationships. As they say, people may forget what you said or what you did, but they will always remember how you made them feel. Personalized follow-ups create those memorable feelings that foster lasting loyalty and genuine connection.

So, as you consider your follow-up strategies, ask yourself: What could you do that would be meaningful to this individual? How can you show that you care beyond the transaction? When you make these efforts, you transform simple business exchanges into opportunities to delight, surprise, and leave an impression that extends far beyond a single meeting.

Surprise & Delight Secret #5:

Celebrate Customer Milestones

Acknowledging a customer's milestones, whether it's a birthday, anniversary, promotion, or even just a significant achievement, is an impactful way to show them they're valued beyond the immediate transaction. It's easy to overlook these moments, but they're key to deepening connections and reinforcing loyalty. When you take the time to recognize someone's special day, it's a reminder that they're more than just another client or business contact—they're an individual with moments that matter.

A simple, handwritten card can work wonders. In a world where digital communication has become the norm, receiving physical mail that isn't a bill or an ad is a rare and pleasant surprise. Consider this: how often do you receive a card outside of holiday times? Probably not often, which is what makes it so special. When I sort through the day's mail, the sight of an envelope addressed by hand instantly brings a smile. It signals that someone put thought into reaching out, a feeling that's both warming and memorable.

When planning to celebrate a customer milestone, remember that it's the personal touch that counts. The content of your card or note doesn't have to be poetic; it just has to be real. A simple "Thinking of you on your special day!" is more meaningful than an impersonal, corporate message. Make it personal by referencing a recent interaction, a project you're collaborating on, or something memorable about them. No matter the message, always make sure it's hand-signed—not stamped—and not typed.

If you decide to send a gift, make it personal. Sending something generic or direct from an online retailer is the easy route—but easy doesn't convey thought. For one, mass-produced items sent directly from a vendor can feel impersonal, like an afterthought. Instead, put a bit of TLC into the process. Wrap the gift yourself or find a vendor who will personalize it with quality packaging, adding a handwritten note to give it a finishing touch. If you know the client has a specific interest, like a favorite type of tea, a sports team, or a hobby, let the gift reflect that. These small details turn an otherwise generic item into a thoughtfully curated experience.

Whenever possible, send the card or gift to the customer's home address instead of their office. I've found that receiving something at home feels far more personal and intimate; it's a gesture that says you thought about them as a person, not just a client. I remember texting a colleague once to ask for his home address to send a little something, and his response perfectly summed up the impact of personalized gestures. He replied, "Whatever you're sending, I appreciate it. I could argue that you don't have to, but I know you well enough by now to know that won't work." This response encapsulates the essence of creating thoughtful experiences—by going above and beyond, you communicate that the relationship itself is what matters most.

There's a fine line between memorable gestures and ones that feel overly scripted. Personalized efforts shouldn't feel contrived or like they were checked off a "client retention" list. The gesture must genuinely feel like it's coming from you as an individual, not as a corporate formality. This might mean occasionally veering away from a cookie-cutter approach and adapting your efforts to each customer's preferences. For some, a carefully crafted email on their milestone might be more appreciated than a card. For others, a small gathering or a celebratory message delivered over coffee might make all the difference.

Consider that people are likely to remember these little moments, especially if they feel celebrated and seen. They'll often keep a meaningful card or memento in a drawer, on a desk, or pinned to a bulletin board as a reminder. A small investment in a card, thoughtful message, or minor gift isn't just about the cost; it's about creating lasting impressions. When they reflect on who remembered their milestone and acknowledged it, it's you and your brand that will come to mind. This type of goodwill generates not just customer loyalty but can also spark word-of-mouth referrals. They might share the experience with a friend or colleague, amplifying the reach of your thoughtfulness.

One of my favorite examples involved a prospective client I had seen speak at an event. During the event, he discussed how he journaled daily and hoped that these journals would one day be a legacy for his children to read. Instead of the usual "It was so nice to see you" email, I took the time to send a personalized journal embossed with his initials. I saw this as an opportunity to show that I'd been listening. He later told me how much he appreciated the thoughtfulness of the gesture, and that journal would be the one he used next. I never did land that client, but I am confident that he remembers where the journal came from each time he pulls it off his shelf.

Ultimately, celebrating a customer's milestone is about creating an experience that feels uniquely tailored to them. People want to feel special, noticed, and appreciated, especially by those with whom they do business. Remember, it's not about how much you spend but about how much thought you put into the gesture. These moments are the glue that holds relationships together, particularly in a world where transactions are often quick and impersonal.

Think of it this way: taking time to recognize someone's special day or achievement is an investment in the relationship. It builds goodwill, demonstrates that you're genuinely interested in them, and goes a long way in setting you apart from competitors who might overlook these moments. In the end, it's these gestures that foster a sense of connection, loyalty, and trust—and in today's world, those are invaluable.

Surprise & Delight Secret #6:

Curate a Mini Experience

Crafting unique, memorable experiences around your product or service can transform a simple transaction into a cherished memory. This kind of intentionality goes a long way in creating customer loyalty and goodwill, and it doesn't always have to be elaborate or costly. The goal is to surprise and delight your customers by offering something exclusive, unexpected, and valuable, which makes them feel appreciated and more connected to your brand.

Imagine a local coffee shop hosting a tasting event where loyal customers can sample new drink flavors before they're released to the general public. The exclusivity and personal touch make customers feel like insiders. These tasting events don't just generate buzz; they make customers feel valued, reinforcing their loyalty in a way that goes beyond the product. They become participants in a private, curated experience, creating a connection that's hard to achieve through conventional customer interactions.

On a more personal note, this concept took on a special meaning when my daughter turned 13. To make it memorable, I coordinated with my three best friends and their daughters for a surprise outing to a P!nk concert. While the concert itself would have been incredible, I wanted to elevate the experience and hired a limo for the night. If you're on my website, www.amplify-experiences.com, you'll see the video of Audrina's reaction when she sees the limo—it was priceless. Sure, it would have been easier (and cheaper) to drive ourselves or call an Uber, but the limo transformed the night from an event into a core memory for everyone involved. Sometimes, it's the "extras" that turn a great experience into something unforgettable.

Kim Perkins, Aimee-Kate Mooney, Lindsay Smith, Audrina Smith, Camryn Perkins, Hannah Perkins, Briana Purcell, Jordyn Perkins and Kristina Purcell outside of the limo en route to the P!nk! Summer Carnival Tour in Philadelphia to celebrate Audrina's 13th birthday.

Likewise, I once attended a vendor-hosted dinner at the Four Seasons in Philadelphia. We had a wonderful meal at a large round table, complete with unique chef creations. But what made this event truly special was a surprise behind-the-scenes tour of the Four Seasons kitchen after dinner. My vendor's husband was a chef at the hotel, and getting to see the inner workings of such a renowned kitchen felt like being granted a secret pass to a hidden world. Even after all the places I've traveled and the experiences I've had, this remains one of the coolest and most memorable moments. It was an unexpected twist that deepened my connection with the host and left a lasting impression.

For those in a business setting, providing a "chef's table" experience is a similar idea, and many high-end restaurants offer this option. The chef's table is often situated in or adjacent to the kitchen, and diners are served a tasting menu with dishes that are often unavailable on the standard menu. It's an experience designed for you and your guests, adding an intimate and exclusive touch that feels truly special. The chef's choice meals can be a delightful surprise, showcasing the chef's creativity while immersing guests in the kitchen's energy.

On a different occasion, I experienced a small yet meaningful gesture when I visited a David Yurman store for the first time. Before I even made a purchase, I was offered a glass of champagne, soda, or water as I browsed the jewelry cases. The refreshments were served on a silver tray, with no pressure to buy. The sales rep spent a full hour showing me different pieces, noting down items I liked but didn't purchase so that I could easily refer back to them. This gesture wasn't exclusive to me; it was available to anyone who entered the store, but it felt thoughtful and personal. Not all retail stores can afford to offer champagne, but a similar level of hospitality could be achieved by offering bottled water or even coffee. Small gestures like this elevate the guest experience, making customers feel special from the moment they walk in.

Creating an experience isn't limited to luxury stores or high-end dining. Take inspiration from pediatricians' offices, which often have a "kiddie corner" with books and toys to keep young patients occupied while they wait. Why can't the same concept exist in a car dealership, clothing store, or bank? Kids aren't only waiting in doctor's offices, and incorporating a kid-friendly area in these other businesses could ease parental stress, making the overall customer experience more enjoyable for everyone involved. A "kiddie corner" with coloring books, toys, or interactive screens can be a simple, low-cost addition that enhances the experience for families.

Ultimately, it's all about going beyond the bare minimum. Think about how you can make each customer interaction feel like a meaningful experience rather than just another transaction. The goal is to create raving fans who will talk about your brand with enthusiasm. In my personal life, this approach has worked wonders; I've now been "hired" by my "nieces" to plan their birthdays for years to come! It's a responsibility I wouldn't trade for anything because these are the moments we all look back on fondly.

The key takeaway? Invest in the unexpected. Whether it's a private tasting event, a behind-the-scenes tour, a curated dinner experience, or simply a thoughtful gesture, these small efforts create an emotional connection that goes beyond products or services. When customers see you going the extra mile to curate a memorable experience, they see that you care about them, not just their business. And in a world where the average consumer is bombarded with choices, that sense of genuine connection is what will set you apart.

Surprise & Delight Secret #7:

Elevate a Traditional Dinner

When planning a client dinner or hosting a special dinner event, it's all about the thoughtful details that set the experience apart. The goal is to make each guest feel as though the evening was curated just for them, turning an ordinary dinner into something memorable and unique. Start by selecting a restaurant that has a distinctive ambiance. The atmosphere alone can contribute significantly to the experience, whether it's a cozy, intimate setting with warm lighting or a chic, modern space with stunning décor. A unique backdrop adds a layer of immersion that makes guests feel like they've entered a different world.

To enhance the experience from the start, pre-order a selection of appetizers for the table. This immediately takes pressure off your guests as they settle in and allows them to enjoy something without having to decide on the spot. Pre-arranged appetizers also subtly convey that you've put thought into their dining experience, providing a warm, welcoming touch that sets the stage for the rest of the evening.

Custom menus can elevate the event even further. Instead of relying on standard restaurant menus, design personalized ones that reflect the occasion. Websites like Canva offer easy-to-use templates that can match the theme or tone of the dinner, whether it's celebratory, formal, or casual. It's an extra step that requires minimal effort but has a major impact—your guests will feel like the dinner was designed specifically for them, not just another reservation anyone could have made.

Hannah's

Appetizers
Cheese & Charcuterie Board
Burrata Display
Passed Arancini

Pizza Station
The Patricio - Pepperoni, Ricotta & Hot Honey
Elm Street - Tomato Sauce & Cheese

Pasta Station
Bucatini with a 'Nduja Vodka Sauce
French Onion Rigatoni

Slider Station
Chicken Parm Sliders
Meatball Sliders
Fries

My niece Hannah's custom menu for her Sweet 16.

If possible, arrange to have a bottle of your client's favorite wine or drink waiting at the table. A signature choice that's been pre-selected demonstrates an understanding of their preferences and shows that you went out of your way to create an experience that's familiar yet exclusive. Work with the restaurant to ensure the bottle arrives before guests order, seamlessly elevating the experience to feel luxurious and personal.

Finally, during the event, focus on creating a relaxed, conversational atmosphere. Ensure that the attention is on them, making each guest feel valued. By anticipating their needs—from the atmosphere and appetizers to the custom menus and special wine—you transform a standard dinner into a curated, memorable experience.

Thoughtful details like these may seem small, but they add up to create a distinctive, high-touch experience. Each one conveys that this is no ordinary dinner, but an event crafted to show genuine appreciation and make your guests feel truly special. These touches don't just leave a lasting impression; they set a standard of excellence that reflects on your brand, building loyalty and connection in ways that are as meaningful as they are memorable.

Surprise & Delight Secret #8:

Teach Your Teams to Problem-Solve

One of the biggest complaints I have about many businesses is that telephones are answered by machines. Now, please don't get me wrong—I am all for technological advancements and enhancements, and sometimes I love being able to go online and search in a chatbot for an answer without having to talk to a soul. But there are times when my need is personal and can't be answered by a computer. There is nothing more frustrating than being stuck in an endless loop of menu selections, trying to get to a real person, only to be disconnected or transferred to a centralized department that can't answer your question.

Think about the experience created when someone answers the phone, and that person has access to the information needed to answer your question. While answering a phone isn't always possible with the size and scope of some businesses, if you can have a human answer, have a human answer. If you can't, make it easy for someone to exit the loop of automated messages when they need to speak to a human.

A few months ago, I needed to buy a new computer. Typically, I would purchase the computer at Staples or Best Buy; however, in this instance, I needed to buy it directly from Microsoft, as they were the only ones with the model I wanted in stock. It seemed like it should be a relatively easy transaction—I chose my computer, added it to my cart, and hit purchase. Much to my surprise, the transaction was unable to go through. I thought perhaps it was a setting on my credit cards or a potential fraud transaction. After some research, I learned the transaction never even got to the bank, so they certainly didn't decline it.

Curious, I reached out to the Microsoft team—first by chat. They let me know there was an issue on their side but assured me it would be corrected in the next couple of hours. I chalked it up to a system glitch. The next day, I tried my purchase again. Same error. I eventually tracked down their number and called someone at Microsoft, who informed me that my account was flagged for fraud because it was trying to purchase a computer. Odd, I know, as Microsoft sells computers. They told me a case was opened and that it would be resolved that evening. This went on for seven days—with seven different chats and customer service reps, each telling me another department was handling it and that I'd be good to go in a few hours. Finally, the last person I spoke with sensed that an unresolved issue wasn't going to sit well with me. They took my information, completed the purchase on their end, and unfroze my account.

I wish I knew why it took seven days and seven different chats for me to buy a computer from Microsoft—and if I didn't need a certain model, I would have stopped trying after the first attempt. I have vowed to never buy a computer from them again and to prohibit my family from doing so. It doesn't matter what their commercials say, or what they send me (which, in this case, was nothing)—it's the frustrating experience that they created. How could it have been better? If the first rep had handled the case like the last rep, I would be singing their praises and talking about how their problem-solving skills helped me with a challenging transaction.

Empower your teams. Let them know they have the ability to problem-solve and to make the customer experience better. And teach them that when they can't, they should follow up to ensure that what they said was going to happen actually did. Experiences aren't just about walking into something grand or being surprised—they're about the manner in which someone speaks to you or works to resolve a problem. Do they add to your life or subtract from it? Would you return to the vendor again based on the transaction or not?

Surprise & Delight Secret #9:

Empower Your Employees to Make it Personal

On an American Airlines flight from Philadelphia to Michigan, I experienced a gesture that transformed the typical flight experience into something truly memorable. As I boarded the plane and found my seat, I noticed a simple piece of copy paper taped above the seat that read: "Welcome Lindsay 4C." This small but unexpected gesture had been made by the flight attendant before I boarded, entirely of her own accord. It wasn't part of her training manual, nor a directive from her supervisors; it was a personal touch she had chosen to add to my experience. This simple, thoughtful note wasn't essential for her role that day, yet it made a significant impact on my perception of American Airlines and my experience as a passenger.

Airlines are typically required only to provide safe, timely travel from point A to point B. Yet, this flight attendant chose to go beyond those basic requirements, offering something that would transform my experience from standard to unforgettable. She knew my name, my seat, and even my status as an Executive Platinum member. There was no extravagant cost associated with this gesture—the paper likely came from her own home, costing nothing to the airline. But by recognizing my loyalty and making me feel genuinely welcomed, she created a moment that left me speechless, ensuring that I would remember—and talk about—this flight with admiration long after the journey was over.

The impact of small, personalized actions like this one cannot be overstated. It highlights the value of empowering employees to fill in gaps and create special moments for customers. This is where a "nice-to-have" gesture, when encouraged and cultivated, can make a business truly memorable. Imagine if all employees had the freedom to find small, unique ways to make customers feel valued. While standardized service has its place, it's these additional touches that linger in a customer's mind and set a brand apart from the competition.

One effective way to foster this culture of personalized service is to empower employees with a small budget dedicated to creating surprise-and-delight moments. Establish a monthly budget for each employee to spend on customer interactions—whether it's a personal note, a small token, or even a few extra minutes of service. This budget allows for meaningful gestures while maintaining control over expenses. Encourage them to share stories of how they used this budget and the reactions they received; these stories will inspire others to do the same, creating a culture of personalized, memorable service.

When customers feel recognized and valued, it builds loyalty in a way that no amount of traditional advertising can replicate. Personal touches, even as simple as a handwritten welcome sign, create a ripple effect, turning routine interactions into standout experiences. These memorable moments become lasting stories that customers like me will share with others, leading to natural, authentic word-of-mouth marketing that can be priceless for any brand.

Surprise & Delight Secret #10:

Follow-Up And Show Appreciation

The post-transaction follow-up is often one of the most undervalued aspects of customer service, yet it can have a profound impact on customer loyalty. A simple call or email after a transaction communicates that the customer's experience matters beyond the sale, showing genuine interest in their satisfaction and leaving them feeling truly valued. It can turn a basic interaction into something memorable and meaningful, fostering trust and loyalty that leads to repeat business and positive word-of-mouth referrals.

Recently, I experienced this firsthand after switching to a new dentist for the first time in 15 years. My first visit included a filling, and the procedure itself was less than ideal. However, the following day, I received a call—not from the office staff, not from an automated survey service, but from the dentist himself. He took the time to check in, ask about my comfort, and ensure that everything was healing well. I was surprised and impressed. His direct, personal follow-up completely changed my perception of the experience and transformed what had been an uncomfortable encounter into a positive one. I felt cared for in a way that a delegated follow-up simply couldn't have achieved.

Consider the impact if more businesses adopted this approach. Often, companies will assign follow-up tasks to office staff or customer service divisions. While this may save time for busy professionals, it can miss an opportunity to deepen the customer relationship. Imagine if the person who had been directly involved in the transaction—the agent, consultant, or service provider—took the time to make that follow-up call. It would communicate that they were personally invested in the customer's experience, not just in closing the sale. This personal touch demonstrates accountability, fosters trust, and shows customers that they're more than just another transaction.

There's immense power in taking responsibility for follow-up interactions. It shows customers that their experience isn't just a box to check off but is a priority for the business. For small businesses especially, this can create a distinct competitive advantage, setting them apart in a world where so many interactions feel automated and impersonal. The follow-up, when done with care and authenticity, can make customers feel like they're not just a client but a valued partner in the business relationship.

Epilogue

In May of 2024, after almost two decades, I left my company. Until the final moments I was there, I continued to live out my passion for creating experiences. The week before I left, I crafted a heartfelt and genuine farewell message to the hundreds of people with whom I had worked and partnered, specifically in the Western Region, which I spearheaded over the last nine years. In response to my departure email, I received many emails, texts, and phone calls from people with whom I had worked who spoke to the power of the experiences we shared together. I keep those notes tucked away in a box—the senders could never have known what they would mean to me.

Looking back, it's clear to me that every intentional action, every small, personalized moment, has the power to leave an impression that lasts far beyond the transaction. I've seen firsthand how a handwritten card, a personalized gift, or a moment of genuine listening can create loyalty and fuel growth in ways no marketing campaign could.

I have proof in the results achieved that you don't need a sales team or cliché marketing efforts to make your brand memorable—you need powerful relationships. Over the years, I was invited to customers' homes, private dinners, sporting events, and outdoor activities. Why? Because they wanted to spend time with me. All of these events were outside of business hours, where clients who became friends chose to spend their time with me not because they had to, but because they wanted to. And that is how you know your brand made an impact.

I am forever grateful that my mom suggested I check out the Kimpton in Phoenix and for Travis's brilliant supersleuth detective work. Without those moments, I might not have been as in tune with the experience and certainly wouldn't have developed the strong alignment with Kimpton that I have today.

With the authenticity of each experience that brands such as Pieri Hospitality and High Mark Distillery create, it is easy to see how their customer experiences transform the spaces they are in, leading by way of community impact, raving fans, and opportunities to showcase innovation. The more ways you find to surprise, delight, and show appreciation for your clients, the more engaged you'll find your customer base. Both Pieri and High Mark have mastered this, and I am honored to have had the opportunity to work with them for so many years to witness firsthand what they are doing with the experience. I am so proud to share them with you.

I am grateful to every single customer, partner, and team member who took a chance on me. My goal was always to make a difference and to impact each of you in some small way on the path to growth—to share a life lesson, to provide for you and your families, to open your eyes to the power of an experience. I know in my heart that I was successful in that mission, and I hope that you carry some of the experiences we had—good, bad, and in between—with you. The reality is that a person and a business can be defined by how they show up in the challenging times. It's easy to be experience-centric when things are good, but innovating and being present when things are bad—that's a testament to a solid brand and relationship.

As you close this book, I invite you to start small—perhaps with a thank-you card, a personalized touch, or an extra moment of care in your next interaction. Every experience you create is a chance to build something lasting, to leave people feeling not only valued but also seen. Together, we can create brands, businesses, and workplaces that don't just serve but truly delight. It starts with just one experience—one memorable moment at a time—and without another company mug.

Acknowledgements

Writing this book has been a journey, one that I could never have completed alone. It truly takes a village—and mine is filled with people whose unwavering belief in me made me believe in myself. For years, being a published author was just a dream on my vision board, something I didn't know how to begin. The task felt overwhelming, like there was always something more important to do. But thanks to the incredible support around me, what once felt out of reach became a reality.

To **Jim**, my business partner and dear friend. Together, we built something extraordinary. You were there, witnessing firsthand the experiences that fueled our region's success and watching as my passion for experiences grew. Thank you for seeing potential in me long before I saw it in myself, for challenging me every day to be more, to do more, and for standing by my side through it all.

To **Felicia** and **Jaime**—our bond is proof of the power that comes when women lift each other up. Thank you for loving me through my hardest days, for listening when I needed an ear, for traveling across the country just to be together, and for always making room for our adventures. Your friendship has been one of my life's greatest gifts.

To **Christina**—the glue that holds Pieri together and now my personal Pilates guru. You've helped me find strength in ways I never knew I needed, and your steady encouragement has guided me through both the physical and emotional challenges along the way.

To **Monica**—you taught me how to diagram a sentence in the 5th grade and convinced me that being messy was a sign of creativity. To this day, I hear your voice in my head every time I correct someone's grammar or obsess over sentence structure. You instilled in me a love of words and precision that has carried me through this process.

To **Aimee Kate**—thank you for always encouraging me to explore my passions, for sitting with me through my emotional storms, and for organizing my chaotic life for so many years. Your steady presence has allowed me the space to create, and I am forever grateful.

To **Freddie**—my coach, mentor, and guide. Your wisdom, gentle nudges, and the way you affirmed my strengths while helping me see where I could grow have shaped me more than you'll ever know. You gave me the courage to take the leap.

To **Stephanie**—my brilliant doctor of "smart things" friend, always diving into every conversation with curiosity and joy. Your infectious energy and thoughtful engagement have inspired me more than words can express.

To **Michael**—for holding down the fort so that I could create experiences that ultimately allowed me to grow in unimaginable ways. Thank you for never stopping me or saying no.

To my **Mom**—your unwavering belief in me, your love, and your support have carried me through life. I wouldn't be here without the lessons you've taught me, the strength you've shown, and the love you've given so freely.

To my **Dad**—you've always been my quiet strength, the one who stands solid no matter the storm. Your quiet encouragement has shaped my journey in ways both big and small. Thank you for showing me that resilience runs deep in our veins.

To my incredible **children, Audrina, Nathan, and Hudson**, you are my everything. Watching you grow, learn, and become the incredible people you are fills my heart in ways I can't even describe. You inspire me every day to be better, to keep pushing, to never give up, and to always keep experiencing.

Each of you has been part of this journey, lifting me up when I doubted myself, cheering me on when the finish line felt miles away, and celebrating with me now that the dream has been realized. Thank you for believing in me. I could never have done this without you.